Joe's Journey

Biden's Rise to Vice President

The News Journal

Introduction

"Joe's Journey" is The News Journal's look at the road traveled by Delaware's colorful U.S. senator, from his birthplace in Scranton, Pa., to his emergence on the Wilmington political scene in the late 1960s to his perch as vice president of the United States.

To compile the chapters of this book, Assistant Managing Editor Greg Burton did original reporting and used material from many News Journal files, some going back half a century. Photo Editor Ron Soliman searched thousands of images for the photographs published here, and Assistant Design Director Jeffrey Cox put it all together in a highly readable format.

Joe Biden has ascended to the highest elected office ever achieved by a Delawarean. He is easily the most recognizable figure in the First State. And he's a character, a man whose memorable statements sometimes reflect enormous political courage, sometimes make you laugh and sometimes backfire.

We had staff members on the ground with Biden in 2007 as he angled for the presidential nomination of the Democratic Party, when he walked away from that quest in January 2008, and when he was announced as Barack Obama's vice presidential pick last summer in Springfield, Ill. We were in Denver for the Democratic convention, in St. Louis for the vice presidential debate, and in Chicago for the president-elect's historic victory speech on Nov. 4.

We chronicled the whistle-stop tour that Obama, Biden and their spouses took in the days before the inauguration, including a stop at the Wilmington train station. And we sent more than a dozen staff to inauguration ceremonies to capture this significant chapter of Delaware's history.

Our talented multimedia staff created a DVD with audio slide shows, hundreds of photographs that didn't make the book, video, and digital front pages from the campaign trail. It's called "Inside Joe's Journey."

Joe Biden has become Delaware's political rock star. "Joe's Journey" helps readers relive his rise to power.

David Ledford
Executive Editor

Curtis Riddle
President & Publisher

Front cover: *Joe and Jill Biden at the Wilmington Train Station during the Inaugural Whistle-stop from Philadelphia to Washington on January 17, 2009.*
Back cover: *The Bidens and Obamas prepare to leave Wilmington.*

 • ISBN 978-0-9639460-2-7

Published by Quebecor World Inc., www.quebecorworld.com. Printed in the United States of America.

Contents

Foreword

By David Ledford

Joe Biden stands behind one of 100 small desks arrayed in a semi-circle on the floor of the U.S. Senate. A group of men and women with stenographic machine bags draped over their shoulders lines up in the blue and beige hall to make a transcript of his remarks, one taking over for the other after several minutes of furious typing while looking directly into Joe's eyes.

To the casual observer, it appears sad that only a dozen or so of Joe's colleagues have gathered to hear the Delaware senator's final speech before assuming his new role as vice president of the United States. But old hands say 15 is an impressive number in the digital age when politicians frequently speak on the floor alone – talking to the cameras of C-SPAN rather than to peers they hope to persuade.

Joe begins softly before raising the timbre of his voice, a strong baritone that bounces off the gallery where his wife Jill, daughter Ashley and son Hunter watch with middle school students, a smattering of reporters and assorted government staffers. His son Beau, Delaware's attorney general, missed this moment because he was returning from Iraq, where his National Guard unit is stationed.

For Joe Biden, this is an opportunity to encapsulate 36 years of service to Delaware and to his country. He begins with a Senate story from 1963, when he was 21 years old. Security was lax then. And Joe Biden the college student was able to drive right up to the Capitol and walk into the Senate. No guards. No metal detectors.

Joe likes the word "literally," and seasons his remarks with it the way some people pour ketchup on potatoes and eggs at breakfast.

"Literally, I walked in. And I walked down here, and I came through those doors," Joe says, motioning to the doors just a few feet behind his desk. "And I walked into the chamber, and the lights were still on. And I was awe-struck. Literally awe-struck.

"And what in God's name made me do it, but I walked up ... and I sat in the presiding officer's chair."

Laughter rolls through the room.

"And I was mesmerized.

"And the next thing I know, I feel this hand on my shoulder, and a guy picked me – a Capitol policeman picks me up and spins me around and he said, 'What are you doing?' "

This is "literally a true story," Joe adds. Ten years later, the same police officer stopped him on his first day as a U.S. senator. The officer asked Biden if he remembered him, but the young lawmaker didn't.

"I welcome you back to the Senate," said the officer, who was retiring two weeks later. "Welcome to the floor legally."

This is the man Delaware has sent to the Senate seven times. He's become a political rock star who President Obama, when explaining to reporters that Joe would lead a national task force on the middle class, introduced as being "the pride of Delaware."

That's literally a true statement, as Joe might say. Regardless of whether you love or loathe Joe, whether you're Democrat or Republican, most Delawareans are proud of the fact that one of their own has risen to vice president.

In the weeks that followed the election, Joe and Jill Biden were applauded when walking into grocery stores, restaurants and other establishments in New Castle County. These outpourings of affection in the produce aisles left Joe "stunned" – and forever grateful.

He has achieved the highest elected office of any Delawarean and today is easily the state's most recognizable resident. It wasn't that way in the beginning.

When Biden first ran for the U.S. Senate 37 years ago, his campaign operated like a small-business startup: His sister Val, his brother Jimmy and his first wife Neilia ran logistics, raised money and organized intimate gatherings statewide where voters were treated to political philosophy, coffee and rolls.

There was an unflinching belief in the product: Joe, an enterprising 29-year-old member of the New Castle County Council who spoke passionately about building a better America, about politicians needing to talk straight and renew trust in government.

Even though young Joey faced the formidable J. Caleb Boggs – a World War II veteran and Republican who had earned labor endorsements, served three terms as the state's lone U.S. representative, two terms as governor and two terms in the Senate – the Biden family was convinced he could win.

"And in the beginning that was enough," Biden says in his memoir "Promises to Keep."

Joe wailed on Vietnam, arguing that the war pushed by President Richard Nixon was wrongheaded, undermining American stature abroad. Slowly, he began closing the 30-point gap in the polls, and he ultimately pulled ahead. An upstart with unwavering faith in himself unseated a towering political figure.

Today, the same kind of superlative can be assigned to Joe. He has spent more of his 66 years inside the Senate than out of it. Working among giants in an institution he reveres, Joe has navigated a river of politics to reach his station as second in command of the U.S. government.

Today a phalanx of police, Secret Service and VP staff members clears a path for Joe wherever he goes. Observant Delaware travelers catching an early train notice idling police cars at virtually every inter-

EMERGENCY EXIT
EMERGENCY EXIT

section some 20 blocks from the station when Joe's caravan is on its way east from Greenville.

Yet when he gets there Joe is the familiar, loquacious Joe. "Hey buddy," he regales men who look familiar but whose names he can't remember. "How you doing, man?"

Joe is a good guy, Bob Jones will tell you. Joe says the same of Jones, a shoeshine man the vice president calls "the mayor" of the train station. They've known each other for years and genuinely appreciate one another's friendship. Joe is as comfortable sitting on a wooden bench with Jones as he is walking the halls of the Capitol.

And the downtown Wilmington train station, with its convenience store, café and ticket offices, has special meaning for Joe. He has commuted by rail during his 36 years in the Senate – an estimated 7,400 round trips between Wilmington and Washington. Train conductor Gregg Weaver says Joe, a tireless advocate for Amtrak, is the system's number one passenger.

When Joe made the historic train trip with President-elect Barack Obama, Michelle Obama and Jill, a trip intended to invoke the spirit of Abraham Lincoln's inaugural ride in 1861, he stepped to a microphone in Wilmington and disclosed a secret: On many days when his car was a few lights away on Lancaster Pike, the train about to pull out, Joe would call conductor Weaver and beg for forgiveness. Miraculously, a mechanical issue would delay commuters a few moments until Joe came aboard.

This is Joe at the pinnacle of his career – yucking it up with the shoeshine man one day, catching a break with the conductor on another. Yet once he slips into his seat on the train, Joe starts thinking about the day ahead, and lately those thoughts have been heavy.

Sitting before a blazing fire in one of the oldest offices in the Senate, his jacket draped over a wingback chair, Joe acknowledges that moving from the legislative to the executive branch of government presents "mammoth" challenges for him personally.

America is fighting two wars abroad and struggling through the worst economic downturn since the Great Depression. Assignments are piling up. Joe is poised to play a significant role in one of the most important chapters of American history.

Asked by a reporter if he can handle it all, Joe, wearing a crisp white shirt and red suspenders, uncharacteristically hesitates a moment while working through his mind the issues that need immediate attention.

"Of course you can," Jill answers for him. "You're Joe Biden."

Joe's staff says he's a workaholic, with 12-hour days routine. Like other executives, he occasionally forgets to eat when consumed by the task at hand. One of the benefits of inheriting the mansion at the old Naval Academy – the house that former Vice President Dick Cheney has occupied the past eight years – is that it will cut down on the commutes, Joe says.

That's a mixed blessing. The train rides gave him time to prepare for the day ahead, Joe says. On the other hand, the vice presidential

Primo Cappuccino
Gate D

mansion, with its gym and private grounds, will afford he and Jill a bit more solace morning and night. It also offers the Bidens a venue for hosting state dinners, as well as events for family and friends.

And should there be a need to return quickly to Wilmington, Joe has a military helicopter at his disposal. His 91-year-old mother Jean no doubt knows her son looks cool in aviator sunglasses, and bounding off a helicopter at New Castle Airport enhances the vice presidential aura.

On the Senate floor, Joe saves the best for last. His farewell speech is a mix of political standup and dramatic reading. His hands are part of the show – slicing the air for emphasis, pounding his chest during a heartfelt moment when he feigns a southern accent, diving into his pants pockets when the story slows down.

When he first arrived in Washington, Joe told Mississippi Sen. John Stennis that he ran for the Senate to uphold civil rights. Stennis was a segregationist, and Joe was embarrassed about speaking so bluntly to a man with an opposite point of view.

Fifteen years later Joe took the office that Stennis had occupied. In their conversation before making the exchange, Stennis lovingly caressed the table that he and other Southerners had sat around while plotting the demise of the civil rights movement.

But the U.S. Senate has a way of changing people, Joe points out. And Stennis told Joe he wanted him to have the table, which Stennis referred to as "the flagship of the Confederacy."

Joe grabs his tie and prepares his mouth for a sudden change of speech. He delivers a Southern drawl with the words of Stennis: "It's time this table passes from the man who was against civil rights into the hands of a man who was for civil rights."

Stennis was in a wheelchair in those days, and the man who had worked against equal rights for blacks turned the chair toward the Delaware senator as he walked out of the office he would soon inherit:

"One more thing, Joe. The civil rights did more, more to free the white man than the black man."

"I looked at him," Joe continues, "I said, 'Mr. Chairman, how's that?' "

Biden slams his open hand against the microphone attached to his lapel as he speaks and exclaims, "It freed my soul. It freed my soul."

It's a poignant moment. The chest beating reverberates through the storied hall.

This layer of Joe's life helps illustrate his point that Congress is made up of people with different cultural and ethnic backgrounds, who worship in different churches and who have different notions about what makes America great.

The next object lesson comes from former North Carolina Sen. Jesse Helms, who came to the Senate the same year Joe arrived.

After hearing Helms berate Kansas Sen. Bob Dole on the Senate floor for supporting the Americans with Disabilities Act, Joe complained to then Majority Leader Mike Mansfield that he couldn't understand how people could be so cruel.

"I can't believe anyone could be so heartless and care so little about people with disabilities," Joe recalls telling Mansfield. "I tell you, it makes me angry, Mr. Leader.

"He said, 'Joe, what would you say if I told you that four years ago, maybe five, Dot Helms and Jesse Helms were reading – I think they were reading The Charlotte Observer, the local newspaper – and they saw an ad in the paper or a piece in the paper about a young man in braces who was handicapped at an orphanage, who was in his early teens.

"And all the caption said was the young man wanted nothing more for Christmas than to be part of a family.

"He said, 'What would you say if I told you Dot Helms and Jesse Helms adopted that young man as their own?'

"I said, 'I'd feel like an absolute fool.' "

Mansfield explained to the young Delawarean that voters send people to the U.S. Senate because there is something inherently decent about them.

"It's easy to find the parts you don't like," Joe recalls Mansfield telling him. "I think your job, Joe, is to find out that part that caused him to be sent here."

This is the larger lesson Joe takes from the institution he loves, and he passes it on with panache: Understand and respect the perspectives of your colleagues, and don't be too quick to judge them.

"Pressure groups can and are strong and important advocates," he reminds his colleagues. "But they're not often, they're not often vehicles for compromise. Personal relationships is (sic) what allows you to go after someone hammer and tong on one issue and find common ground on the next.

"It is the grease that lubricates this incredible system we have."

Joe gets a standing ovation when his remarks end. Sen. Hillary Clinton of New York, tapped by the president to be secretary of state, is about to give her farewell address and a new group of senators is walking onto the floor.

People file by to hug Joe and shake his hand. He returns their embrace, flashing his trademark smile. And making his point on the value of personal relationships, Republican Sen. John McCain of Arizona, who months earlier lost his presidential bid to Obama in a tough campaign in which he and Joe took many shots at one another, makes his way to Joe's desk.

Lions of the Senate fasten grips on each other's shoulders and share a heartfelt greeting.

The is the ointment generated from a long personal relationship. And Joe's going to need a lot of it to navigate his vice presidency.

Chapter 1: Inauguration

"On this day, we gather because we have chosen hope over fear, unity of purpose over conflict and discord."

— President Barack Hussein Obama
during his 2009 inaugural address

His wife Jill awakened him from a deep sleep.

The results for the Iowa caucuses were coming in, and it looked worse than anyone had expected.

It was Jan. 3, 2008. Joe Biden had decided to take a nap as results were tallied. Before he drifted off, he was full of energy and enthusiasm. He had pledged to stay in the presidential race through the end of the month, "no matter what."

But Jill woke him and told him the bad news. They discussed their options.

Instead of preparing to move on to New Hampshire with the other candidates, Joe Biden found himself behind a microphone in a cramped room, giving an emotional concession speech to tearful family members and supporters, his final quest to be president squashed in a cold Midwestern conference room.

The media, the national attention, moved on without him.

"I knew for him it was the end of a journey," said senior adviser and speechwriter Mark Gitenstein.

Just over a year later, Biden stood on the steps of the U.S. Capitol. Six feet away, Barack Obama had his left hand on Abraham Lincoln's velvet Bible and was repeating the words of Chief Justice John Roberts. More than a million people stood on the National Mall. A cold wind blew across them, steam puffed from their mouths. Frigid souls on marble steps and concrete walkways, and a world community linked by live digital video, paused to see Obama, the first black president of a nation founded by slaveholders.

The National Mall had been the scene of other signature American moments, inaugurations of John F. Kennedy and Franklin D. Roosevelt, the Nation of Islam's Million Man March, the "I Have a Dream" speech by the Rev. Martin Luther King Jr., and the rally to end the Vietnam War.

A year after one of the lowest points in his career, Joe Biden is sworn in as the 47th vice president of the United States by Associate Justice John Paul Stevens with wife Jill at his side.

All of those seemed a prologue to this: the inauguration of President Obama on Jan. 20, 2009.

Joe Biden was first, laying his hand on an ornate, century-old family Bible that he had used each of the seven times he was sworn in as a Delaware senator. "Quite a Bible, huh?" Biden asked Associate Justice John Paul Stevens, who administered his oath. After finishing, Biden leaned close to Stevens, smiled and thanked him. He turned to kiss Jill as his children, Hunter, Ashley and Beau, joined the circle around the 47th vice president.

Obama swore his oath next, joined by his wife, Michelle, and daughters Malia and Sasha. Presiding over a nation torn by war and worry, Obama pledged to restore unity and hope, mixing political pragmatism with more lyrical flourishes about a nation that "cannot prosper long when it favors only the prosperous." It was an electric moment. A few in the crowd surrounding the West Front of the U.S. Capitol shouted, "Yes, we can," danced with American flags, raised their hands to the heavens and cried.

"Forty-four Americans have now taken the presidential oath," Obama said during a 19-minute speech crafted more to sober than to exalt. "The words have been spoken during rising tides of prosperity and the still waters of peace. Yet, every so often, the oath is taken amidst gathering clouds and raging storms. At these moments, America has carried on not simply because of the skill or vision of those in high office, but because 'We the People' have remained

Despite the frigid cold, Barack Obama's swearing-in as the nation's 44th president was an electric moment, striking emotional chords with the more than 1 million people who packed the National Mall. In his inaugural address, Obama spoke of restoring unity and hope to a nation torn by economic crisis and foreign wars.

faithful to the ideals of our forebears, and true to our founding documents.

"Today I say to you that the challenges we face are real. They are serious and they are many. They will not be met easily or in a short span of time. But know this, America – they will be met."

The vice presidency, a first for a Delawarean, seemed a fitting capstone for Biden, who first went to Washington in 1973 to fight for civil rights. His new position beside Obama brought him full circle.

"It's almost as profound, it sounds ridiculous to say, as if I got elected," the two-time presidential candidate said in an interview a week before the inauguration. "But this is more historic."

Obama was just shy of 3 years old when the Civil Rights Act passed in 1964. Except for a momentous speech in March at Philadelphia's National Constitution Center, he did not make race a focal point of his campaign. The son of a Kenyan father and a white mother from Kansas, Obama inspired hope among supporters of his campaign by promising a change from the Bush administration. He drew inspiration from Lincoln.

Obama did not face the disintegration of the Union that Lincoln most feared. The rebellious Confederate States of America had formed and inaugurated Jefferson Davis as its new president two weeks before Lincoln's inauguration. Rumors swirled that assassins would stop Lincoln before the oath was complete. And a few weeks later, the nation would be engulfed in its bloodiest conflict.

Obama was barely out of law school in 1995 when Doris Kearns Goodwin started work on her widely acclaimed book "Team of Rivals," which explores the "political genius" of Abraham Lincoln. Now, the 2005 book will be among those in the Oval Office. His selection of Biden and New York's Hillary Rodham Clinton as secretary of state – both of whom were campaign opponents – led many to say Obama was engineering a Cabinet like Lincoln's.

Lincoln wanted the strongest, most able leaders in the country working with him, Goodwin said. Though he had no pro-slavery voices in his circle of advisers, he had a "great range of opinions" about how to handle slavery.

Obama was determined to invoke Lincoln at every turn. Facing the Lincoln Memorial, Obama and Biden took their oaths three weeks before the bicentennial of the birth of Lincoln. The inaugural theme, "A New Birth of Freedom," was inspired by the Gettysburg Address. Three days before the inauguration, Obama took a whistle-stop train ride from Philadelphia to Washington, tracing the last leg of Lincoln's weeklong train ride in 1861 from Springfield, Ill., through Indiana, Ohio, Pennsylvania, New York and on to Washington. The train carrying Obama and his family picked up the Bidens in Wilmington, where both men gave a speech at the Amtrak station on the banks of the Christina River. Obama pledged to work for the "quiet heroes," the blue-collar workers, nurses and teachers "who need change."

On the National Mall, tens of thousands huddled on marble steps and hung on railings for a glimpse at the inauguration of the first black U.S. president.

Overleaf left: *In his inaugural address, Obama said: "We will fight for you every single day that we're in Washington, because Joe and I are both committed to leading a government that is accountable, not just to the wealthy or the well-connected, but to you."* ***Overleaf right:*** *President Obama and Vice President Biden descend the Capitol steps with their wives after the swearings-in for the ceremonial review of the troops.*

"We will fight for you every single day that we're in Washington, because Joe and I are both committed to leading a government that is accountable, not just to the wealthy or the well-connected, but to you."

The menu for the post-inaugural lunch in the U.S. Capitol's Statuary Hall – with seafood stew, pheasant and duck with chutney, and apple cinnamon sponge cake – was based on the tastes of Lincoln. At the luncheon, Obama whispered into the ear of Massachusetts Sen. Ted Kennedy, who attended despite battling a brain tumor. Kennedy later suffered a seizure and was rushed by ambulance to a hospital. He was released the next day.

After the luncheon, crowds from the National Mall shifted to the parade route along Pennsylvania Avenue. The 56th Presidential Inaugural Parade featured Delaware groups among 13,000 participants from 50 states, including Delaware State University's 110-member Approaching Storm Band, the Delaware Volunteer Firemen's Association, Alexis I. du Pont High School's marching band and the University of Delaware Fightin' Blue Hens marching band. The Obamas and Bidens walked a few blocks as thousands, leaning out of balconies or standing along the avenue connecting the Capitol and the White House, cheered. The Obamas took a limousine to the White House, popping in for a brief look before emerging to watch the rest of the parade from a reviewing stand.

Joe Biden walked most of the parade route, soaking up the love. With the U.S. Capitol as his backdrop, he blew kisses and beamed as the crowd shouted, "Joe, Joe, Joe!" He raised his hands, prompting more cheers, and pointed and waved up high and down low. He spotted a Delaware flag hanging from a balcony, and with arms outstretched, gave the shouting crowd a special thumbs up.

"How cool is that?" said one of the parade announcers, laughing. "The vice president out walking the route. We salute you."

That prompted a little jogging spurt from Biden.

"And running the route!" the announcer said.

Smiling and waving by his side were Jill, chugging along in black-heeled boots, Ashley, Hunter and Beau, Delaware's attorney general who returned from National Guard service in Iraq for the ceremony. Leaving behind a warm vice presidential limousine, they braved the freezing temperatures, walking past the White House toward the Executive Office Building – Biden's new office – clearly enjoying every bit of the moment.

After the parade, Obama and Biden and their wives retired from the cameras, changed clothes and bounded among 10 inaugural balls celebrating the military, Washington neighborhoods and regions of the United States, with special balls for Obama's home states of Illinois and Hawaii and Biden's of Pennsylvania and Delaware.

The next day, for the first time in three and a half decades, Joe Biden started a new job. He awoke at the vice president's home, No.

In brief remarks at the inaugural lunch, which included senators, Supreme Court justices and former presidents, Biden praised his former colleagues, and then Obama: "Mr. President, you've inspired a nation," he said, calling Obama "my new boss."

Overleaf: *The Obamas walked a few blocks of the inaugural parade, but Biden walked most of the route, blowing kisses and offering a special greeting to a group with a Delaware flag.*

1 Observatory Circle, not at home in Greenville. No conductor was there to hold the train just a minute or two so "Amtrak Joe" could make it to the platform. While Biden said he would give Obama his unvarnished opinion, his role often would require public silence, something that would be an adjustment for the orator whose farewell speech from the Senate lasted 40 minutes.

Biden planned to spend three out of four weekends in Delaware, where his mother Jean will continue to live. He worked out special arrangements with the Secret Service so that his trips to Happy Harry's and church don't become an "embarrassing" event.

Asked what he thought his election to vice president meant to Delawareans, Biden said, "In a bizarre sense, more than it means to me. I have been stunned, literally stunned, at the response."

Biden wasn't eager to leave the Senate, his "second family." His friendships there developed and deepened amid life tragedies – the loss of his wife Neilia and daughter Naomi in an accident just after he was elected in 1972 and surgeries for brain aneurysms that nearly took his life. He grew up in the Senate, having been first elected just before his 30th birthday, making him the sixth youngest senator ever to serve.

But Obama changed the equation. As one longtime adviser told Biden: "How, if he looks at you and asks you to be vice president, can you say 'No' to an African-American nominee ... without making a lie out of everything you've done, you've worked for?"

Joe Biden's first day as vice president culminated with 10 inaugural galas. ***At right:*** *Biden, son Beau, daughter Ashley, son Hunter and Jill at the Home States ball.*

580EX

Chapter 2: Man from Scranton

"I worked like hell. Practice, practice, practice. I would memorize long passages of Yeats and Emerson, then stand in front of the mirror in my room on Wilson Road and talk, talk, talk."

— Sen. Joe Biden on overcoming a childhood stutter in Scranton, retold in his book "Promises to Keep: On Life and Politics"

Joe Biden was born in Scranton, Pa., on Nov. 20, 1942, to Joseph Robinette Biden Sr. and his wife, Jean.

Joe Sr. was a car dealership manager; Jean was a homemaker. An Irish-Catholic family, they were staunch Democrats living in a neighborhood where politics were as vital as water and coal.

Former Pennsylvania Gov. Bob Casey and his son, U.S. Sen. Bob Casey, a contemporary of Biden's, grew up a few blocks away. Hugh Rodham, Hillary Clinton's father, was born in the city. His father, an immigrant descended from Welsh coal miners, worked in a Scranton textile mill. Rodham is buried in Scranton's Washburn Street Cemetery, not far from the headstones of some of the 110 men and boys who suffocated in 1869 when a shaft fire cut off their escape from the Avondale coal mine.

Clinton was born in Chicago, but growing up she spent her summers at the family cabin in Lake Winola, near Scranton and the Susquehanna River. Proud of its history of millworkers and miners, laborers and unions, and a two-fisted work ethic, Scranton's Democratic Party fell in love with its adopted daughter, who carried nearly three-fourths of the city on her way to a win in the April 2008 Pennsylvania primary.

When Clinton dropped out of the race in June, Arizona Sen. John McCain and Barack Obama sharpened their focus on the state's 21 electoral votes. The candidates returned often to the swing state, courting voters hit hard by home foreclosures, job losses and Wall Street's savaging of pension funds and 401(k) savings. Obama's selection of Biden, hailed for his foreign policy bona fides, solidified the ticket's hold on Pennsylvania's electoral riches.

Introducing Biden as his choice for vice president to a crowd in Springfield, Ill., Obama said Biden "is still that scrappy kid from Scranton who beat the odds; the dedicated family man and committed

Joe Biden visits his hometown of Scranton on Sept. 1, 2008. Biden's middle-class upbringing was referenced frequently during the campaign.

Catholic who knows every conductor on that Amtrak train to Wilmington. That's the kind of fighter who I want by my side in the months and years to come."

A town of about 125,000 when Biden lived there in 1950, Scranton was a good place to be a middle-class kid. Though jobs have disappeared and its population has shrunk to about 74,000, not much else has changed. The city's St. Patrick's Day Parade is still one of the biggest in the country.

The Bidens lived in Green Ridge in a five-bedroom vernacular Colonial built in 1929. When young Joe lived there from 1942 to 1952, he slept in an attic bedroom that overlooked North Washington Street, which stretches two miles through downtown Scranton, past shuttered factories and aging mansions of erstwhile coal barons before reaching Green Ridge's modest homes.

As a child, struggling to overcome a severe stutter, he wrote "Joe Biden was here" on a wall inside the home.

Lined with shade trees, Green Ridge is one of Scranton's most desirable neighborhoods, where most residents are Catholic and Irish. Even after the Bidens moved to Delaware, the family came back to Scranton on weekends and summers as Joe, his sister and two brothers grew up. Biden opens his 2007 book, "Promises to Keep: On Life and Politics," by recalling the frequent visits to the town of his birth.

"The first principle of politics, the foundational principle, I learned in the 1950s in my grandpop's kitchen when I was about 12 or 13 years old," Biden wrote. "My parents had recently moved us to Delaware, but most

Biden, with sister Valerie and younger brother Jimmy, played on his town's first Little League team. Decades later he returned to relive some of those memories. As a child, Biden recited poetry into a mirror to overcome a severe stutter. During seven terms in the Senate and on the campaign trail, he often spoke in front of huge crowds and large television audiences.

CHANGE
WE NEED
WWW.BARACKOBAMA.COM

Friday nights Mom and Dad would load me, my sister Val, my brother Jimmy and the baby, Frankie, into our car and drive up to Scranton, Pa., to spend the weekend at grandpop Finnegan's house."

His father was born in Baltimore and raised in Wilmington. His mother's family lived in Scranton for generations. Biden's great-great-grandfather was an engineer who laid out many of the city's early streets. Jean Finnegan, 91 when Obama and Biden won the 2008 election, lives on property near Biden's home in Greenville, Del.

In speeches and interviews on the campaign trail in 2008, Biden emphasized Scranton's values of perseverance, family and faith.

"The Finnegans were a very close-knit family who treasured good relationships and friendships," said Tom Bell, one of Biden's close childhood friends, who still lives in Scranton. "They were just a tight family and a good family. And that was how they raised their children."

Biden and Bell attended St. Paul Catholic School, where Sister Eunice had nicknames for both of them. Biden was "Bi-Bi-Blackbird" because of the stutter; Bell was "Sleepy-eyed Bell" because he had trouble staying awake.

Those were formative years. On a visit to Scranton a couple of years before the 2008 election, Biden showed up at the Green Ridge Little League field after dark, just to look around and remember. In 1951, he played on Green Ridge's first Little League team.

Hillary and Bill Clinton campaigned with Biden in Scranton on Oct. 12, 2008. Clinton's father Hugh Rodham was born in Scranton and Hillary spent summers nearby. ***At right:*** *Grandpa Finnegan holds Joe and Valerie. Biden got his first lessons in politics in his grandpop's kitchen.*

"It was at least 10 o'clock because we'd already turned all the lights out," said Ron Kroptovich, a Little League coach. They quickly flipped the lights back on, and Biden, who was with old friends, tossed some balls around and took photos with Kroptovich's children.

At Hank's Hoagies, the corner store where Biden and his friends used to buy penny candy, the senator signed a photograph that sits framed on the counter: "You make me feel at home again," he wrote.

"We're all Irish-Catholic Democrats," said Tommy Owens, who grew up in the Green Ridge neighborhood and bought Hank's 11 years ago. The size of someone's living room, and unadorned with the fixtures of modern convenience stores, Hank's is known as a place to talk politics, where customers grab a cup of coffee and a stool.

A sign hanging behind the counter defines the Irish Way: "Now don't be talkin' about yourself when you're here. We'll surely be doin' that after you leave."

Scranton nurtured the brand of intimate politics that Biden perfected in the Senate. The handshake, the nod, the close grip and grin.

Less than a month before the November election, Alaska Gov. Sarah Palin drew more than 5,000 to Scranton's Riverfront Sports Complex. In Biden's trips to Scranton, he spoke to a couple of hundred here, 10 or 20 there, or one or two in a living room, courting voters like good neighbors. On one visit before joining Obama's ticket, he surprised Anne Kearns, a retired art teacher and grandmother who bought the Biden home with her husband in 1962.

"I was on my way to the grocery store and up pulls this big SUV, and Sen. Biden starts walking up," Kearns said.

"I said, 'Sen. Biden!'

"He said, 'You know me?'

"I said, 'Of course I know you!'

"I think everybody in Scranton knows about Joe Biden."

He's never stopped coming home.

A childhood friend said Biden's family was known as being close-knit. "They were just a tight family and a good family. And that was how they raised their children." Biden often emphasized perseverance, family and faith, values he says he learned in Scranton. At right, Biden signs autographs after a campaign stop in Scranton.

Chapter 3: Pigskin to Politics

"In 1970 I told my wife I thought I'd like to run for New Castle County Council. I explained it was a GOP district, so I probably wouldn't win, but I'd learn a lot, which had to be a good thing for somebody who wanted to make a more serious run later."

— Joe Biden, in "Promises to Keep"

Joe Biden was shaving in a motel sink when the knock came.

Dover's Hub restaurant and motel was on the corner of Loockerman, near Dover Downs, a harness racing track and stop on the NASCAR circuit. A popular watering hole and political hangout, the Hub was close enough to the state capital's loftier haunts that a young Biden picked the motel as his base for the state party convention.

In 1971, Republicans controlled the governor's office, both Senate seats and the state's only House seat. The Democrats were in disarray and July's convention included shouting matches over Vietnam, abortion rights and legalizing marijuana. Biden, in his first elected post, was fighting irrelevance as the GOP carved up his New Castle County Council district, adding Republican voters and subtracting Democrats.

He was young then – a fresh face for Delaware, a strapping law school graduate with a ready smile and a dream to "do great things and earn a place in history books." But victory in 1972 seemed doubtful.

In his underwear, Biden answered the knock to find Party Chairman Henry Topel and former Gov. Elbert Carvel. The two men sat down on a polyester bedspread and asked Biden to run for the U.S. Senate against Republican incumbent J. Caleb Boggs. Biden put on his pants and told them he'd think it over. He talked to Neilia Hunter, his first wife, his mom, Jean, pop Joe.

The Bidens had planted deep roots in Delaware since the move two decades ago from Pennsylvania to the Claymont development of Brookview Townhomes. Biden attended Holy Rosary School before enrolling as a high school freshman at Archmere Academy in 1957. He sent three children to the same school, Joseph "Beau" Biden III, elected Delaware's attorney general in 2006, Hunter and Ashley.

Biden, who now lives in Greenville, returns to the working-class town

Football in hand, Joe Biden boards a plane in Manchester, N.H., on Sept., 10, 2008, off to another stop on the campaign trail. Football was a big part of young Biden's life. He starred for three years at Archmere Academy in Claymont, Del., and played on the freshman team at the University of Delaware.

Nearly 50 years after his high school career ended, former teammates remember one thing about Biden: Even though he wasn't the biggest or fastest or strongest player, he was the one they counted on to make the big play.

of 16,000 people to attend its annual Christmas parade. In his autobiography, Biden describes the strong Catholic tug, and his "Oz": Archmere, the former country estate of John J. Raskob, the onetime DuPont executive, board chairman at General Motors and campaign manager of New York Gov. Al Smith. In 1928, Smith was the first Irish Catholic to claim the presidential nomination for a major party when the Democrats backed him.

The Norbertine Order bought the estate in 1932, turning it into a Catholic preparatory school. The architecture and the opulence appealed to Biden, a decent student who gained his first small measure of fame playing football for Archmere. He wasn't the biggest player. Or the fastest. Or the strongest. But if you threw a football anywhere in his vicinity, he would catch it. That's how former teammates remember Biden, nearly 50 years after his senior year, when he was part of an undefeated season at Archmere.

"He was the most talented receiver I ever had," said John Walsh, who was in his first season as the Auks' coach in 1960. "We threw a lot to him. He had soft hands. He was able to catch anything thrown to him."

Football, and sports in general, have played an

important role in Biden's life. Athletics helped him overcome a stutter that affected his confidence. But at the University of Delaware, Biden chose love over football, quitting the team before his senior year so he could spend his weekends driving to Syracuse, N.Y., to court Neilia, a student at Syracuse University.

"As much as I lacked confidence in my ability to communicate verbally, I always had confidence in my athletic ability," Biden wrote in "Promises to Keep." "Sports was as natural to me as speaking was unnatural. And sports turned out to be my ticket to acceptance – and more. I wasn't easily intimidated in a game, so even when I stuttered, I was always the kid who said, 'Give me the ball.' "

In Biden's final high school game, Archmere played at Friends Central in Philadelphia. Both teams were undefeated. The Auks had a big lead with just a few minutes left in the game when quarterback Bill Peterman, who later played at the Coast Guard Academy, gathered the offense in the huddle.

Biden wrote that Peterman told them that this was their final chance to score in their high school careers, and that he would divvy up the chances among the four main senior ball-carriers. Peterman decided that Biden would get the first crack at it. Biden looked at him and said: "OK, I'll take it first. But you're not getting the damn ball back, Peterman."

Biden, number 30, scored the winning touchdown in his final game to secure an undefeated season at Archmere. "The most talented receiver I ever had," said his coach, John Walsh, right.

"I must have run 110 yards, zigzagging from sideline to sideline, but I wasn't going down until I got to the end zone."

"That was Joe," said Mike Fay, Biden's teammate at Archmere. "He always wanted the ball."

Biden played halfback at the University of Delaware. The freshman Hens played against other college freshman teams and preparatory schools. The team had limited contact with the varsity, which then was coached by Dave Nelson, who had a young assistant named Tubby Raymond, now a UD coaching legend.

On spring break of his junior year, Biden went to Florida and then hopped a plane to the Bahamas, where he met Neilia. Biden spent weekends over the spring and summer driving to upstate New York to visit, joining her in 1965 as a first-year law student at Syracuse.

Biden's football days ended there, though he tossed a football around during the 2008 campaign, squeezing the pigskin as he climbed the steps to board a rented plane destined for Iowa, New Hampshire, Montana, Florida, Ohio, Pennsylvania and Delaware.

After law school, Biden set up shop in Wilmington. Then came a pivotal moment – Biden's first run for political office. In 1970, he campaigned for a seat on New Castle County Council, and won. Just a year after passing the Delaware bar, Biden entered politics on a platform in support of affordable housing in the suburbs.

His storied run for the Senate came two years later. In a tumultuous political climate, President Richard M. Nixon convinced Boggs, who died in 1993 at age 83, to seek another term, ending the senatorial aspirations of U.S. Rep. Pete du Pont, and leaving the door open for a vocal upstart like Biden, as brash as he was unknown.

His sister, Valerie Biden Owens, ran the campaign. Together, they courted the same sort of middle-class voters Biden grew up with in Scranton and Claymont, although in 1972 the neighborhoods were mostly Republican.

"Val had run every campaign I was in, and she would manage my Senate campaign too," Biden wrote in "Promises to Keep." "The race for Senate was risk-free. Only a handful of people outside the family thought I had a real shot to win, so I figured even if I lost, people were going to say, 'That's a nice young guy.' I was confident I could be a solid candidate. And I actually believed I could win."

With little money and nothing to lose, Biden edged Boggs on Nov. 7, 1972, by 3,162 votes. The stunning win was Biden's first incredible moment as a young politician with promise. He would be the sixth-youngest person to serve in the Senate, following Tennessee's John Henry Eaton, who was 28 in 1818, Virginia's Armistead Mason, 28 in 1816, Henry Clay of Kentucky, 29 in 1806, Rush Holt of West Virginia, 29 in 1934 (he took the oath after turning 30) and Delaware's other young Senator, William Wells, 30 in 1799.

Neilia's dad gave the couple the down payment for a second house in Washington, D.C. The kids would go to school down the street.

Joe Biden leads a rally outside Hotel du Pont in 1972, the year he upset two-term Republican incumbent J. Caleb Boggs for the U.S. Senate.

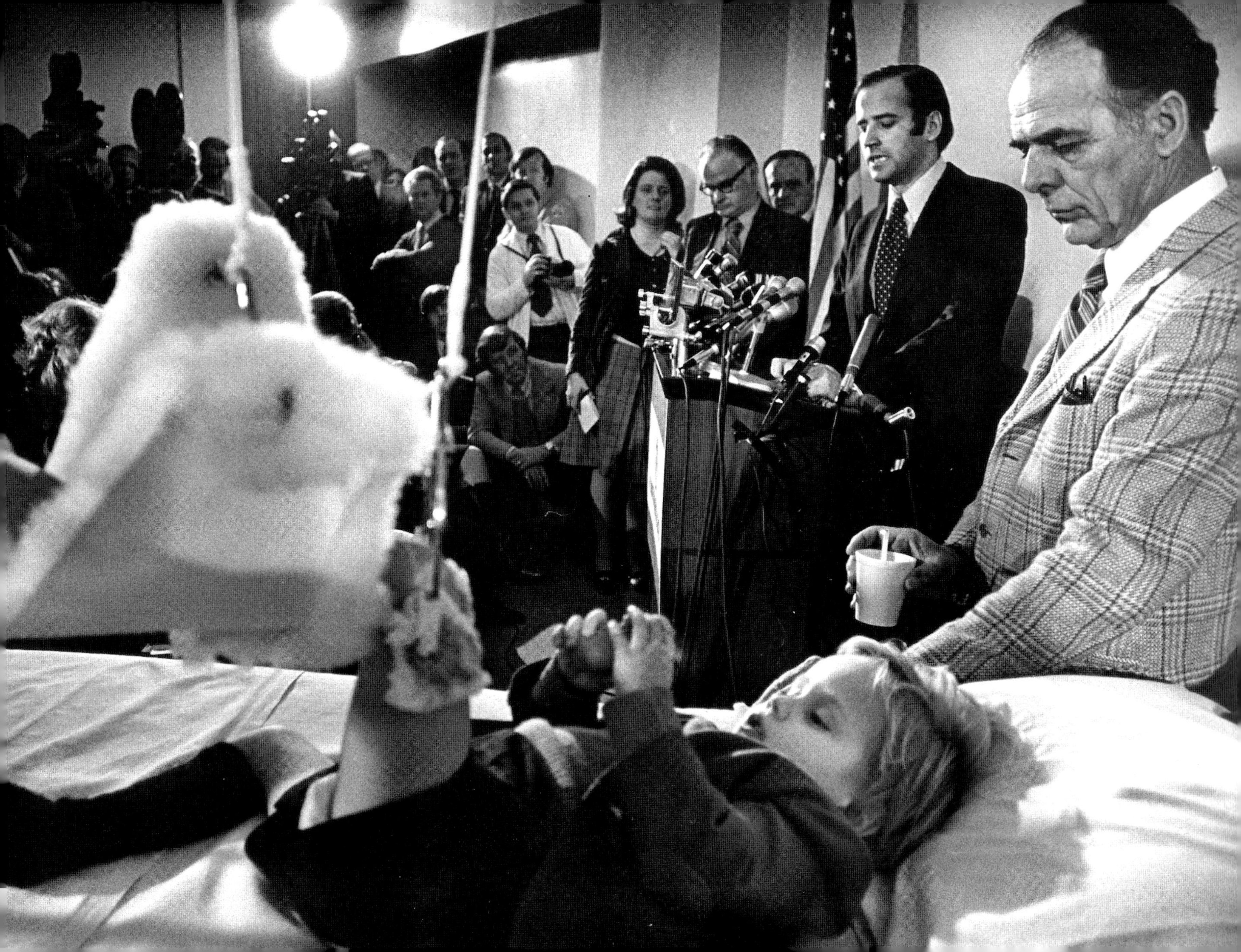

Chapter 4: From the Ashes

"Most of all I was numb, but there were moments when the pain cut through like a shard of broken glass. I began to understand how despair led people to just cash it in; how suicide wasn't just an option but a rational option. But I'd look at Beau and Hunter asleep and wonder what new terrors their own dreams held, and wonder who would explain to my sons my being gone, too. And I knew I had no choice but to fight to stay alive."

— Joe Biden in "Promises to Keep"

The call from the White House came on Dec. 19, 1972.

"Mr. President, Sen.-elect Biden for you," a secretary intoned.

President Nixon was patched in, but Biden uttered the first words.

"Hello, Mr. President. How are you?"

A day earlier, Biden's wife Neilia and daughter Naomi were killed when the family's Chevrolet station wagon collided with a tractor-trailer loaded with corncobs at Valley and Limestone roads near Hockessin, Del. His young sons, 4-year-old Beau and 3-year-old Hunter, survived but suffered serious injuries.

Biden was on Capitol Hill at the time. Neilia was shopping for a Christmas tree.

"I know that this is a very tragic day for you, but I wanted you to know that all of us here at the White House are thinking about you, and praying for you, and uh, and also for your two children," Nixon said in a brooding baritone captured on a tape released in December 2008 by the Nixon Presidential Library.

"I understand that you were on the Hill at the time and your wife was just driving by herself."

"Yes, that's correct," said Biden.

A political life may have ended there if not for Senate Majority Leader Mike Mansfield, a Montana Democrat who befriended the suddenly single father of two young boys. Biden told Mansfield that he planned to relinquish his seat in the Senate, but Mansfield

After the accident that killed his wife and daughter, Joe Biden had to be convinced to take his place as a U.S. senator. He was sworn in on Jan. 3, 1973, from the hospital room of his sons Beau, shown, and Hunter.

encouraged him to reconsider, calling him repeatedly as the young senator-elect stood vigil over his sons' hospital beds.

An Irish-American, like Biden, who grew up in Montana coal country, Mansfield appointed Biden to the Democratic Steering Committee, a plum for a freshman senator. Biden relented and took the oath of office from his sons' hospital room. He told Mansfield he'd try it for six months. Faced with a tragedy that would cause most people to retreat from daily life, Biden did the opposite. He reached out to family, friends and supporters. He offered words of comfort and talked about his grief in an outspoken manner that would define his career.

Photos of the accident show the family station wagon reduced to a pile of twisted metal and broken glass. Biden wasn't expected to attend a memorial service for Neilia and Naomi at St. Mary Magdalen Catholic Church in Talleyville. But he came and stood in front of a crowd of about 650 and spoke candidly about his "two girls."

"Things were just too good ... something had to happen," he said. "The night before she died, she was writing Christmas cards. We were both in the living room in front of the fire and I was sitting in my lounge chair, a pompous young senator thinking about the big things I was going to do in Washington."

Neilia had earned a master's degree in education and taught English after college. "She had a principle – she treated everyone the same and that worked both ways," Biden said at the memorial service. "Those who were poor, black, minority, affluent or socially esteemed, she made no distinction among them. I was probably one of those phony liberals ... the kind that go out of their way to be nice to a minority, and she made me realize I was making a distinction. ... I'm going to be that way. ... I'm going to try to follow her example."

The accident curved the trajectory of Biden's life. He was in Washington interviewing prospective staff members the afternoon of the accident. Neilia was to meet him there the next day so they could finalize the purchase of a house. Instead, Biden remained in Wilmington, commuting to Washington for the work day, beginning the affair he has since nurtured with the incessant roll of the trains that connect Wilmington with Philadelphia and Baltimore and Union Station, the last stop before the Russell Senate Office Building, Pennsylvania Avenue and the White House.

Amtrak's depots were Biden's campaign stops, the bench seats and tabletops of the Metroliners and Acelas his mobile headquarters, his connection to East Coast coffee vendors and newspaper hawkers, to corporate commuters and tourists from the heartland. As a senator, the railroad tracks were his link to Beau and Hunter, a pipeline to family, friends and fatherhood.

The accident changed Biden's outlook. Instead of maintaining a residence in Washington, Biden commuted back and forth from Wilmington so he could tuck his young sons into bed each night. When Obama announced Biden as his running mate, he said, "Out of the heartbreak of that unspeakable accident, he did more than become a senator – he raised a family."

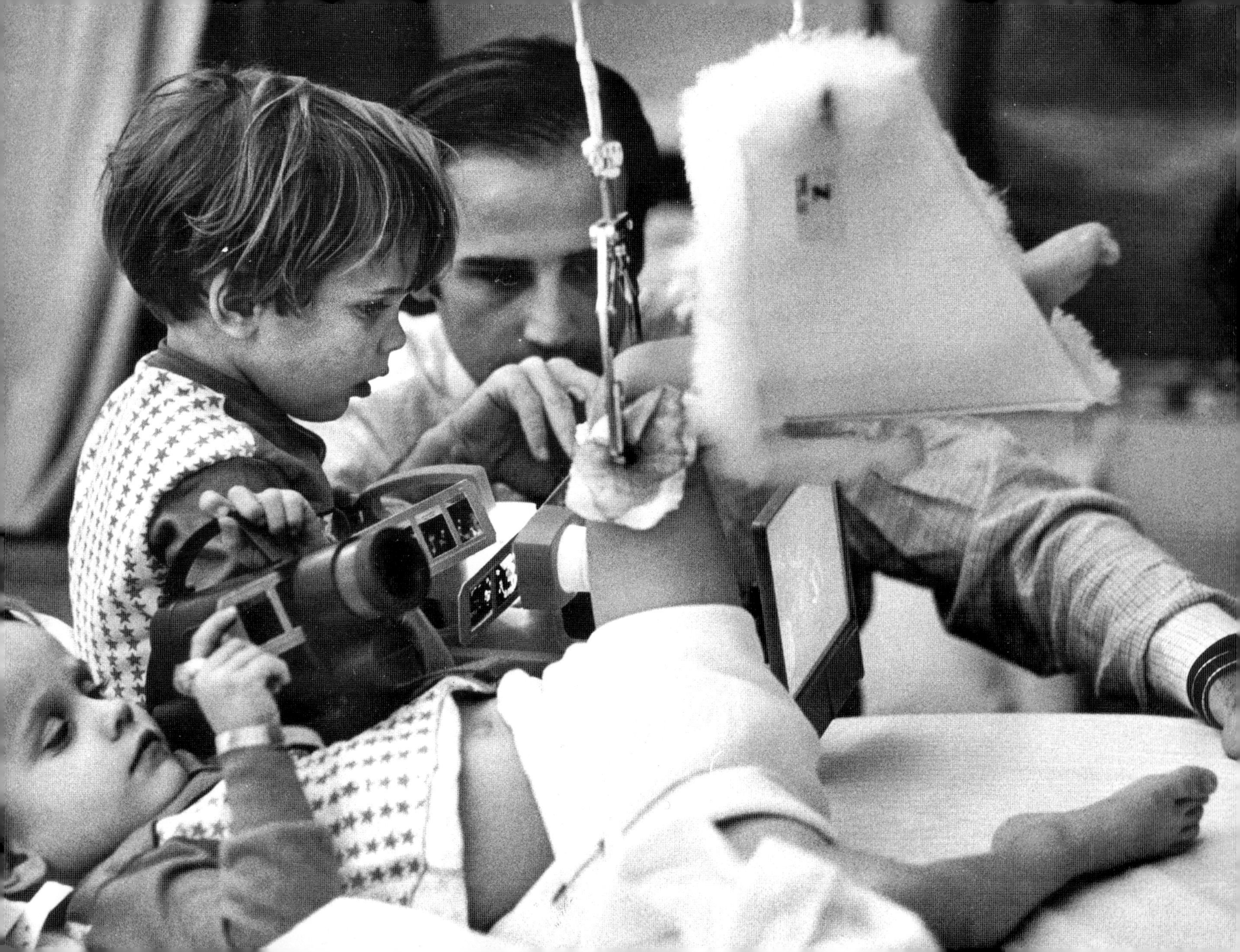

SEPTA
269

In Washington, he took refuge in the Senate. Giants like Mansfield, Hubert Humphrey, Ted Kennedy and Robert Byrd protected him. "Without any fanfare in late December, in a cold driving rain, (Byrd) drove to Wilmington, Delaware, stood outside at a memorial service at a Catholic church for my deceased wife and daughter – got soaking wet in that cold rain. Never once came to see me. Just to show his respect. Got back in the automobile and drove back to Washington, D.C."

Introducing his running mate on Aug. 23, 2008, in Springfield, Ill., Obama recounted Biden's story for the world: "Out of the heartbreak of that unspeakable accident, he did more than become a senator – he raised a family. That is the measure of the man standing next to me. That is the character of Joe Biden."

In the short arc of a phone call, Nixon saw in Biden the promise of his own, long since spent, youth.

"I mean looking at it as you must in terms of a future because you, you have the great fortune of being young," Nixon told Biden. "I remember I was two years older than you when I went to the House. But the main point is, you can remember that [Neilia] was there when you won a great victory and uh, you enjoyed it together. And now I'm sure that she'll be watching you from now on. Good luck to you."

On Jan. 3, 1973, still keeping vigil over Beau and Hunter, Biden took his first Senate oath at their bedsides.

His train commutes gave Biden and his staff time together to strategize. "The good thing about the train is that I'm seldom not prepared. My staff has gotten it down to a science of giving me one hour and 20 minutes of reading down and back."

Chapter 5: Lion of the Senate

"The truth is, in 1992 it was up to the United States to lead. As long as there is one good actor in the world, every other nation can play at the margins. Every other nation can act out of realpolitik and the basic decency in the world won't collapse. But when every country is acting with nothing but self-interest in mind, it's a much more dangerous world."

— Joe Biden addressing U.S. involvement in Yugoslavia in "Promises to Keep"

Skimming over the mountains of Afghanistan, Joe Biden wondered if the Black Hawk could land in a snowstorm.

At about 10,000 feet, with shrinking visibility, the pilot turned back toward Bagram Air Base. Alongside a treeless slope, Biden watched the sharp cliff edges blur into the fast-moving storm. "This was a snow squall that just came in like 'bang.' It went from clear to no visibility at all."

A small road came into focus and the Army pilot dropped out of the sky.

The emergency landing prolonged a weeklong trip in February 2008 to Afghanistan, India, Turkey and Pakistan. Biden and two other senators had been flying for about an hour and a half in the Kunar Valley in eastern Afghanistan before the storm hit. They had been trying to reach Tora Bora, the region where Osama bin Laden was said to have hidden in caves when the United States attacked the Taliban in 2001.

As the Black Hawk touched down, about a dozen Afghans looked up from a tiny village. F-15 fighter jets were deployed to patrol the skies until a seven-vehicle convoy reached the area, two and a half hours later. Biden and Sens. John Kerry, D-Mass., and Chuck Hagel, R-Neb., hiked about 15 minutes to reach the escort. Together, the men marched down the snow-covered mountain in the dark.

Snow seemed a tame distraction to the trouble Biden faced flying in and out of Iraq more than a dozen times after Sept. 11,

Joe Biden, chairman of the Senate Judiciary Committee, and Ted Kennedy confer during Robert Bork's confirmation hearing in 1987. Biden presided over the hearings for Bork and Clarence Thomas, two of the most infamous in history.

UNHC
The UN

2001. On one flight, the anti-missile system on a C-130 cargo plane engaged. Another time, a bullet zipped by his helicopter as Biden neared Baghdad's Green Zone.

In the late stages of his Senate career, wars in Iraq and Afghanistan, Bosnia and Yugoslavia consumed Biden. Black Hawks and C-130s became as routine as Amtrak trains for the chairman of the Senate Foreign Relations Committee. As the vice presidency neared, Delaware's senior senator resisted surrendering control of the strategic committee, hanging onto the chairmanship until just five days before the inauguration.

Before reciting his final Senate oath to Vice President Dick Cheney on Jan. 6, 2008, Biden worked the Senate chamber, shaking hands and chatting. Jill, his wife of more than 30 years, stood near. The former Jill Tracy Jacobs of Willow Grove, Pa., she raised Beau and Hunter as her own and gave birth to Biden's daughter Ashley nine years after the death of his first daughter, Naomi.

For the Irish boy from Scranton and Claymont, the Senate opened a window to the world. Biden, a constitutional scholar, spent decades forging his political career in the heat of international conflict. He has met leaders of nearly 60 countries, territories and international organizations, among them nine Israeli prime ministers, four Soviet leaders and two Russian presidents, Pope John Paul II and the Dalai Lama. He has spoken with Iraqi leaders Iyad Allawi, Ibrahim al-Jaafari, Nouri al-Maliki and Jalal

As chairman of the Senate Foreign Relations Committee, Joe traveled the world, often to war zones. At left, Biden speaks to a man from Chad during a UN-sponsored trip to the country on May 31, 2005. Above, Biden shows federal housing officials a newspaper detailing poor living conditions in Laurel, Del., while fighting for federal funds in 1973.

Talabani, Egyptian Presidents Hosni Mubarak and Anwar Sadat, Libya's Muammar Qaddafi, Queen Elizabeth of the United Kingdom and South Africa's Nelson Mandela.

In his 36 years in the Senate, Biden cast more than 12,000 votes. He is the longest-serving senator in Delaware history and among the longest-serving senators in U.S. history. Biden played a major role in developing anti-crime legislation, including the Biden Crime Law in 1994 and the Violence Against Women Act, a landmark anti-domestic violence law. As chairman of the International Narcotics Control Caucus, Biden also wrote the legislation creating a national "drug czar" to oversee U.S. anti-drug policies.

In large measure, Biden's success has been due to his ability as a curbside campaigner. His reputation is to shoot from the hip, as he did in 2004 when he called President George W. Bush "brain dead" while campaigning for Sen. Kerry. Republicans were outraged by his comments, but since Biden had also called former Democratic President Bill Clinton brain dead, many people dismissed the GOP's criticism. Biden revived the line against President Bush on July 4, 2007, during a campaign stop in Des Moines, Iowa.

As chairman of the Senate Judiciary Committee, Biden presided over two of the more infamous hearings in its history – those of Robert Bork and Clarence Thomas, both of whom had been tapped for seats on the U.S. Supreme Court. Thomas, despite claims that he sexually harassed staff members, made it to the nation's highest court. Bork, a darling of conservative Republicans, did not.

Fresh off the national exposure he had received from the Bork hearings, Biden sought the 1988 Democratic nomination for president but withdrew when he was accused of using portions of British Labour Party leader Neil Kinnock's speeches without attribution. Biden had made the proper attribution in previous speeches but said he had forgotten to do so during an appearance at the Iowa State Fairgrounds. A recording of the speech led to charges made by aides to former Massachusetts Gov. Michael Dukakis, who eventually won the Democratic nomination but lost the race by a landslide to the first President Bush.

On the night of the 1988 Iowa caucuses, Biden gave an unremarkable speech in Scranton on the Intermediate-Range Nuclear Forces treaty, signed two months earlier by President Ronald Reagan and General Secretary Mikhail Gorbachev, but awaiting Senate ratification.

Hard knocks had not crushed Biden. He'd been in the Senate for 15 years. He'd rebounded from the death of his first wife. With his sister Valerie's help, he thrived as a single father, and when he met Jill, a senior at the University of Delaware, Beau and Hunter took part in the courtship.

In Ramadi, Iraq, on Sept. 6, 2007, Joe Biden talks with Marine leaders before a meeting with Iraqi and American government officials and Sunni sheikhs.

The first of five daughters, Jill was raised by a stay-at-home mom and a banker dad, Bonny and Donald Jacobs. On Jill's first night out with Joe, he ended the date with a handshake at her door.

Jill called her mother at 1 a.m. "Mom, I finally met a gentleman."

Biden had seen her photo in a public art display and told his brother, who knew Jill from UD, he'd like to date her. She didn't think they would have much in common, but went out with him to learn about his life. After that, they saw each other nearly every night for two years. But Biden had to ask Jill five times to marry him. Knowing their union would make her a stepmother to two boys who had lost a mother and an infant sister in a car accident made her cautious. "It was Joe, the boys and the state of Delaware, and I had to take my time."

After they married in 1977, Jill gave up her high-school teaching job to raise the boys and Ashley, the daughter she and Joe had in 1981. As the kids grew, Jill returned to teaching and upkeep at a former DuPont Co. mansion Biden bought near the Hagley Museum in Greenville.

Then-Vice President Dick Cheney poses for a ceremonial swearing-in for Joe Biden's seventh Senate term. Biden was the youngest person sworn in to a full seventh term. Fourteen days later, after resigning his Senate seat, Biden took the oath of office to succeed Cheney.

"It's the kind of place a thousand Italian guys died building – hand-carved doorways, a curving hand-carved grand staircase that Clark Gable could have carried a girl down, a library fit for a Carnegie, or Bernard Baruch, someone like that," Richard Ben Cramer wrote in his 1988 book "What It Takes." "Joe found it one night, a couple of years after he became a senator. He was driving around, like he did back then. He was snooping around Greenville, streets of his dreams, when he saw it, all overgrown, boarded up. Some developer was going to knock it down. ... He got in the developer's face and started talking – fast."

Jill was in Greenville on the night of the Iowa caucuses. In Scranton, Biden watched Missouri Rep. Dick Gephardt take first, edging out Sen. Paul Simon of Illinois and Dukakis.

The following night, Biden spoke at the University of Rochester. He felt good about the audience and his answers to questions about the Bork hearings, Iran-Contra, Reagan and Gorbachev, and his reasons for dropping out of the presidential race. But he felt strange.

For months he'd worked through headaches and shooting pain in his shoulder. A doctor in Delaware thought it might be a pinched nerve. He kept a bottle of Tylenol handy. After the Rochester speech, he sat down on the edge of his bed in a hotel room. His mind drifted, and then he collapsed. Five hours later, he woke up on the floor. He and a friend took a plane back to Wilmington and in Greenville he climbed into bed but his family got him up and took him to St. Francis Hospital. An artery in his brain was leaking. A Catholic priest read last rites.

Tests at Walter Reed Army Medical Center near Washington, D.C., showed a large berry aneurysm at the base of the left side of his brain. With a metal clip, surgeons stemmed the bulging artery. A blood clot in a lung complicated recovery and three months later surgeons repaired a second, smaller aneurysm on the right side of his brain. The consummate Senate man would be gone from the chamber for seven months.

"As I heard it, my chances of surviving the surgery were certainly better than fifty-fifty," he wrote in "Promises to Keep." "But the chances of waking up with serious deficits to my mental faculties were more significant."

Biden dropped weight and wore a ball cap to cover the staples and scar on his head. He found it hard to read, and focus. Facts and names escaped him and the possibility loomed that his voice could vanish.

But the Bidens, with Jill in the mix, rallied around him. To make sure he rested, they screened calls from Ted Kennedy until Kennedy showed up at the door. Many thought the combination of health problems and the plagiarism charges would be too much for him to overcome, that his career was over.

Chapter 6: Iowa, 1988 and 2008

"In 1987 I couldn't yet visualize myself doing the job of president, but by the end of that campaign I could picture in my head how I'd get the nomination. When I started to campaign in 2005, it was the reverse. Doing the job I could see. I was absolutely prepared for that. But I wasn't yet entirely sure how to get my message through the media din that surrounds voters."

— Joe Biden in "Promises to Keep"

Pumped up on adrenaline, Joe Biden compared himself to an athlete as he stood under bright lights at the Polk County Convention Complex on game day – the 2008 Iowa caucuses.

As he put it, he was the punt returner. The ball was about to be snapped. "I don't think about being tackled. I think about scoring." The same focus carried the teenage Biden to the end zone for Archmere Academy, to Syracuse law school from Scranton, and to the U.S. Senate, at just 29, from the modest post of councilman for New Castle County.

In Iowa on Jan. 3, Biden was confident he would at least beat New Mexico Gov. Bill Richardson, despite trailing him in most polls. A surprise fourth-place showing, if close, would lend legitimacy and public support to his campaign, propelling him into the debates and finally opening donor floodgates.

He chartered a jet to leave that night for the next contest, five days later in New Hampshire, and said he would at least stay in the race until the Jan. 26 primary in South Carolina and the Jan. 29 contest in Florida, "no matter what."

Half an hour later, the early evening caucuses began.

Dramatic highs and lows have long been a part of Biden's personal and political narrative. At campaign events, he recounts his father's advice for tough times: "Champ, when you get knocked down, get up!" That message has been the engine of his life. In Iowa, 20 years after his first presidential run collapsed, feverish Democrats were ready to pick Biden back up.

Much had changed since his first foray into national politics. The glare of the Bork hearings had faded, his old precinct network had been

Joe Biden started Jan. 3, 2008, thinking he was a serious contender for president. Later that night, as the results of the Iowa caucuses became clear, he abruptly withdrew from the race.

BIDEN
PRESIDENT
WWW.JOEBIDEN
I'm a Health Care Voter!
BIDEN
PRESIDENT

invaded by Obama's youthful volunteers and YouTube cheerleaders. In 1987, he was one of the Democratic front-runners, beginning his campaign at the Wilmington train station with a rousing speech from the back of the "Biden Express."

"It would be a wide-open field in 1988 – no incumbent and no heir apparent on the Democratic side," Biden wrote in "Promises to Keep." "I was pretty sure the most formidable Democrat, New York's governor, Mario Cuomo, wasn't going to run. And when I took a look at likely candidates – Gary Hart, Richard Gephardt, Jesse Jackson – I felt I measured up. I was just forty-two years old, but after a decade on the Senate Foreign Relations Committee and nearly that long on the Senate Select Committee on Intelligence, I knew the world and America's place in it in a way few politicians did."

Surviving Iowa this time would be as treacherous as the first time.

Two decades later, the Iowa State Fair's butter cow and greasy food on a stick still mattered, but the crush of media spun every word and gesture. Bloggers with grainy video trafficked in off-the-cuff remarks, and Biden's blunt style, appealing and unsettling, attracted more heat than light.

Early in the campaign, Biden said he wasn't worried about being a liberal Yankee in South Carolina because Delaware "was a slave state." When he announced his presidential campaign on "The Daily Show with Jon Stewart," he apologized for calling Barack Obama the "first mainstream African-American who is articulate and bright and clean and a nice-looking guy."

But Biden also got positive press at the South Carolina Democratic Party's Path to the Presidency debate, with his one-word answer – "Yes" – to a question about whether he would have verbal discipline on the world stage. As the caucuses approached, the crowds grew. Biden rated well on national television and in Iowa's living rooms and kitchens.

In 2007 and 2008, Joe Biden campaigned in Iowa for months in the hopes of pulling out a fourth- or even third-place showing. Twenty years earlier, right, he campaigned there as one of the Democratic front-runners.

World events also broke his way. A week before the caucuses, a resurgent Benazir Bhutto was assassinated in Rawalpindi, Pakistan. President Pervez Musharraf and other world leaders turned to Biden for advice and counsel.

The media started making note of it, with some saying a Biden surprise showing was possible. His aides called the buzz "Mo Joe." Short on resources, Biden relied on the national exposure of his chairmanship of the Senate Foreign Relations Committee and his charm sparring with television pundits on the Sunday morning news shows. On the ground, he ran a traditional campaign, focusing on Iowans who had been to previous caucuses and were likely to show up.

"They knew I had no money," he said, "because they knew I made no promises."

In Des Moines, the Biden campaign set the scene at their rally with photos of Biden on the campaign trail flashing on a movie screen and music that included Tina Turner singing "Simply the Best."

As the caucus ended and the adrenaline faded, an exhausted Biden fell asleep.

The two-and-a-half months he spent campaigning in Iowa were all to meet a comparatively modest goal – a surprise third- or fourth-place finish. But as election results delivered the state for Obama, frustrated Biden supporters gathered in a 4,100-square-foot room. When Biden finished fifth, not even able to muster a percentage point, most blamed the Obama onslaught.

A debate on Dec. 13, 2007, less than a month before the Iowa caucuses, featured John Edwards, Barack Obama, Bill Richardson, Hillary Clinton, Biden and Christopher Dodd. By the beginning of February, only Clinton and Obama were still in the race. Months of flipping burgers and shaking hands in Iowa yielded a fifth-place finish for Biden, who did not register a single percent of the vote.

Jill woke him before the post-caucus party and they ended the campaign as they began it – with a family decision. Supporters at the Science Center of Iowa waved signs in a dimly lit room and shouted, "We love you."

"I love you guys, too," he said, with more than a dozen family members, some tearful, standing behind him. He sounded paternal. "I fell asleep until it was over. I shouldn't admit that to you, but I did. As I got up and Jill told me the results, I feel no regret. Not one single solitary ounce of regret.

"Let me make something clear to you. I ain't going away."

Biden die-hards chanted. "Joe, Joe, Joe, Joe ..."

Leaving the stage, he hugged his way through the crowd and headed to a brightly lit side room. He looked tired, but sounded upbeat. Delaware Gov. Ruth Ann Minner later called to cheer him up but they both ended up in tears. "I could tell he was choked up and crying and he said to me, 'I feel so bad for my family. ... They were so excited and all of a sudden there's nothing,' " Minner said.

Biden arrived at that crushing moment after a humbling battle for media attention against a field of celebrities and a struggle for cash so profound he had to share a plane with another presidential candidate, Connecticut Sen. Chris Dodd. After his concession speech, Biden said he didn't expect the record turnout or that so much of the vote would be consumed by the front-runners.

"If I care about what I say ... I should get back to the Senate and try to keep people's feet to the fire, try to make the changes I've talked about," he said. "I feel good about what we did, I feel good about the race we ran. I'm going to keep it up. I'm going to go back to the Senate, and I'm going to go back and thank the folks in Delaware for giving me the grace period to come out here and try this."

Biden said he entered the race – his last for the White House – because he thought it was the right moment for him.

On the campaign stump, Biden told audiences how he grew up with foreign leaders, pitched his plan for a political settlement in Iraq and talked of restoring America's place in the world.

In a race that focused on change versus experience, Biden told audiences that he had both. But, too often, his knowledge of foreign affairs left some audience members talking not about his qualifications for president, but his qualifications for secretary of state.

During a post-caucus interview, Biden said, "No, no," when asked whether he would take a position as secretary of state, but then seemed to leave the door open to a position in the new administration. "I'd have to be convinced that the nominee, the Democratic president, we really shared the same kind of views."

Biden rattled off a list of upcoming Senate hearings on Iraq, Pakistan and Africa. Then, he boarded the plane chartered to New Hampshire and headed to his home in Greenville, instead. "There's a lot of work to do, and I hope I can play a very constructive role."

Biden had said his 2008 presidential run would be his last for the White House. After dropping out, he barely left the door open to taking a position in a new administration.

IDEN
ESIDENT '08
WWW.JOEBIDEN.COM
BIDEN
PRESIDENT '0
JOEBIDEN.C
DEN
DENT
ENT '08

CHANGE
WE CAN
BELIEVE IN

Chapter 7: Super Sunday

"If you will stand with me on Tuesday and vote for me on Tuesday ... and keep the dream alive for those who still hunger for justice, I promise we will not just win Delaware or Super Tuesday or the nomination or the general election, but we will change this country and transform the world."

—Barack Obama, in Rodney Square on Sunday, Feb. 3, 2008

On this chilly morning in Wilmington, Market Street was a madhouse.

Barricades choked off foot traffic. Cars were turned away. Police escorted residents to and from their homes at the Residences at Rodney Square, a high-rise apartment building overlooking the green. There was tension, but no Molotov cocktails. No curfews, rocks or rifles. No National Guard troops or police patrolling black neighborhoods, silencing young, idealistic men with handcuffs, escorting them out of Rodney Square like they did here in 1968.

The young black men on Market Street this day, among 20,000 people pushing into Wilmington's Colonial town square, were anticipating the speech of another black man with a message of hope and change, not mourning the bloody remains of an earlier dream.

Many were surprised by Barack Obama's Sunday visit to delegate-poor Delaware. Two days later, on Feb. 5, 2008, 22 states would make their presidential preferences known in the Super Tuesday primaries and caucuses. Hundreds of delegates to the national nominating conventions were at stake, and convincing wins on Tuesday could propel Obama to the ballot in November.

Joe Biden had conceded a month ago in what was now a contest of wills between Hillary Clinton, buoyed by a win in New Hampshire, and Obama, whose genius lie in merging the lyrics of history with the rhythms of politics.

That's why many believed he chose this pivotal day to come to Wilmington's Rodney Square. Nearly 40 years earlier, violence in Rodney Square spilled from the edges of a memorial service for Martin Luther King Jr., assassinated in Memphis on April 4, 1968.

Two days before Super Tuesday, in which 22 primaries were contested, Barack Obama, left and overleaf, stood among thousands in Wilmington's Rodney Square. Forty years before, tension following Martin Luther King Jr.'s assassination sparked rioting and National Guard occupation of the city.

OBAMA'08
OBAMA'08

More than 400 people in Wilmington would be arrested over the next several days. Dozens of families were left homeless from fires.

Though the violence in Wilmington would subside within a week, a nine-and-a-half-month occupation by the National Guard, which numbered 3,500 at times, would last until January 1969. Guardsmen weren't put on the streets to keep the peace for that long anywhere else in the country, even though King's death sparked violence in cities from coast to coast. Wilmington's occupation remains the longest of a U.S. city since Reconstruction ended in 1877.

When the first rock crashed through a window, Biden was finishing law school in Syracuse. "Downtown Wilmington was a strange place at the end of 1968," he wrote in "Promises to Keep." "The city had been under martial law for nearly six months. The Democratic governor, Charles Terry, had called out the National Guard when rock and bottle throwing escalated to sniping, looting, and arson in the days following Martin Luther King's assassination. ... In the black neighborhoods of East Wilmington, residents were afraid, too. Every evening National Guardsmen were prowling their streets with loaded weapons. Curfews were in effect from dusk to dawn. Mothers were

This memorial service for Martin Luther King Jr. in Rodney Square soon percolated into violence leading to perhaps the darkest time in Wilmington history. Days of rioting, fires and hundreds of arrests led to the longest occupation of a U.S. city since 1877. Forty years later, Barack Obama drew 20,000 people and spread his message of hope.

terrified that their children would make one bad mistake and end up dead. ... The nightly news had a way of making these stories seem like a conversation between the races in Wilmington, but I knew blacks and whites weren't talking to each other."

Obama thrived on such symbolism.

Standing before Caesar Rodney's nearby statue, Obama said the Delaware patriot "stood up to the British Empire" and rode through a thunderstorm on the night of July 1, 1776, to break a deadlock in Philadelphia over the signing of the Declaration of Independence. Obama cited the "Greatest Generation," which struggled to defeat the Axis powers during World War II, and women who fought for the right to vote.

"That's what hope is – imagining, then fighting for and struggling for what did not seem possible before," he said. "This is the moment we are in right now in Delaware and across the nation."

Before speaking to the crowd, Obama met briefly at the Hotel du Pont with his five co-chairs – Lt. Gov. John C. Carney Jr., State Treasurer Jack A. Markell, Mayor James M. Baker, Wilmington City Council President Ted Blunt and Insurance Commissioner Matt Denn. The November election propelled Markell into the governor's office and delivered Baker, Wilmington's second black mayor, into a historic third term.

Kamryn Jackson, 8, was among 20,000 people who filled Rodney Square and surrounding streets for Barack Obama's Feb. 3, 2008, rally.

On stage before Obama's speech, Markell quoted a verse from the Bible's Book of Hebrews: "Faith is the substance of things hoped for, the evidence of things not seen."

"Faith," Markell said, "is what has brought us here."

Gov. Ruth Ann Minner skipped the speech, having endorsed Hillary Clinton. Though Obama complimented both men in his early remarks, neither Biden nor Sen. Tom Carper attended.

Baker said it was logical for Obama to visit Wilmington. "We're the meeting ground. We're near New Jersey, Maryland, Pennsylvania. ... And he can bring us back to being Americans, instead of being conservative or liberal. I don't support a candidate just because he's African-American, but because he is the best of the candidates."

It was the largest gathering in Wilmington since Vice President Lyndon B. Johnson visited Fort Christina Park. Thousands who couldn't reach the town square mingled on Market, King and 10th. Stephanie Sherrer walked about a mile from her Madison Street home with son Joshua Malave and daughter Xena Malave. "I wanted them to have this experience and see this history. I'm excited about a black man being in the running and I'm also excited about a woman." Her son, Joshua, then just 10, said he'd tell his "children I saw this dude Obama and then my children will tell their children."

Littleton Mitchell, former head of the state NAACP, called Obama's visit a point of hope, weighed against decades of prejudice and oppression in Delaware. "Sen. Obama coming is a good idea, but I have reservations. I do not believe that this country has progressed far enough in its democracy to permit either a woman or black man to be president."

Mitchell articulated a fear shared by many: Obama would be targeted, just like King. "I know that anyone can be eliminated at any time. I hope he is well protected."

Three days before Obama ignited Rodney Square, his wife Michelle brought thousands of supporters to their feet during a pair of rallies in Wilmington and Dover. A crowd at The Grand in Wilmington was predominantly black and female in a contest punctuated by race and gender. "They said that he was too black. They said that he wasn't black enough. When all that didn't work, they threw in a fear bomb – they said his name is funny. We have heard it all."

At Delaware State University organizers had to turn away hundreds who wanted to be near the wife of the Democratic hopeful. The capacity crowd at The Grand was six times larger than any Michelle Obama had previously spoken to on the campaign trail. Dressed in a dark-gray pinstripe suit with a plum blouse, she leaned her tall frame slightly forward as she spoke bluntly and without notes.

"I believe in my heart that this race has nothing to do with whether Barack is ready. That's not even an issue. The question is whether you're ready."

Organizers turned away hundreds in Dover trying to see Michelle Obama days before her husband drew thousands to Rodney Square.

Chapter 8: 'A More Perfect Union'

"I am the son of a black man from Kenya and a white woman from Kansas."

— Barack Obama in a March 18, 2008, speech at the National Constitution Center

For more than a year, Barack Obama had escaped attempts to color his candidacy in black and white. But criticism over his former pastor's racially charged sermons forced Obama to redirect his stump speech from the message of unity to an examination of our country's deep-seated divisions.

Hillary Clinton was demonstrating a vitality that shook Obama's calm, methodical momentum. Arizona Sen. John McCain was moving to the right to unite his party's base, and YouTube video once again proved influential by spreading the inflammatory words of the Rev. Jeremiah Wright, son of a Baptist minister from Philadelphia, to the homes of American voters.

Wright, a member of the campaign's African-American Religious Leadership Committee, had said in 2003 that the government gives blacks "the drugs, builds bigger prisons, passes a three-strike law and then wants us to sing, 'God Bless America.' No, no, no, God damn America, that's in the Bible for killing innocent people."

Cable news devoured the unearthed clip. Wright's patriotism, and by extension Obama's, were challenged, adding hype to false reports that Obama was a Muslim. Wright stopped consulting with the committee and retired from Chicago's Trinity United Church of Christ in February 2008, a month before Obama's March 18 speech.

Not scheduled to be with him, Michelle Obama rushed to Philadelphia. With the National Constitution Center, and the symbolism of the nation's founding document, as a backdrop, he delivered the most important speech of the campaign. The pivotal Pennsylvania primary was five weeks away.

"I am married to a black American who carries within her the blood of slaves and slaveowners – an inheritance we pass on to our two precious daughters," Obama said. "I have brothers, sisters, nieces, nephews, uncles and cousins of every race and every hue, scattered across three continents, and for as long as I live, I will never forget that in no other country on Earth is my story even possible. It's a story that

Obama's patriotism was called into question because of a former pastor's inflammatory rhetoric and misinformation about Obama's religion. As issues of race threatened to derail his campaign, he stepped to the microphone at the National Constitution Center in Philadelphia and delivered the most important speech of the campaign.

hasn't made me the most conventional candidate. But it is a story that has seared into my genetic makeup the idea that this nation is more than the sum of its parts – that out of many, we are truly one."

Obama had written about his ancestry in two books before the campaign, and then left it mostly behind. Others weren't so inclined. Early in the contest, President Bill Clinton said his wife might lose the Jan. 26 primary in South Carolina because of race, drawing a sharp rebuke from the Obama camp, but also renewed attention to the dormant prejudices of suburban voters in the Rust Belt and the uglier passions of the South.

A week before Obama came to Philadelphia, Geraldine A. Ferraro, the Democratic vice presidential candidate in 1984, left Clinton's campaign after suggesting Obama wouldn't be where he is today if he were white. Then, with the race for the presidency turning nasty, Wright's years-old description of the United States as fundamentally racist compelled Obama to dig deeply into America's roots.

Obama said Wright spoke for a generation that grew up with legalized discrimination, a lack of economic opportunity and the segregated "reality" of the '50s and '60s. Anger, hidden from white co-workers and friends, suppressed in public, could creep into the otherwise praiseworthy rhetoric of the pulpit. "We would be making the same mistake that Rev. Wright made in his offending sermons about America – to simplify and stereotype and amplify the negative to the point that it distorts reality."

Similarly, white Americans may see affirmative action as a punishment for a crime they never committed. "Like the anger within the black community, these resentments aren't always expressed in polite company. But they have helped shape the political landscape for at least a generation."

Not scheduled to be with her husband in Philadelphia, Michelle Obama rushed there to hear his speech. It proved to be one of the turning points of the Democratic primary. Seven months before Obama's Philadelphia speech, the Rev. Jeremiah Wright appeared in Wilmington at Mother African Union Church. The occasion was August Quarterly, a celebration started by church founder Peter Spencer in 1814.

Refusing to turn his back on his longtime pastor, Obama said Wright is "like family to me" and a more spiritual leader and tolerant person than the clips on "endless loop" on YouTube and news networks have depicted.

"I can no more disown him than I can disown the black community," Obama said. "I can no more disown him than I can my white grandmother ... a woman who loves me as much as she loves anything in this world, but a woman who once confessed her fear of black men who passed by her on the street."

Obama condemned Wright's words, but not the message. "The profound mistake of Rev. Wright's sermons is not that he spoke about racism in our society. It's that he spoke as if our society was static; as if no progress has been made; as if this country – a country that has made it possible for one of his own members to run for the highest office in the land and build a coalition of white and black, Latino and Asian, rich and poor, young and old – is still irrevocably bound to a tragic past. But what we know – what we have seen – is that America can change. That is the true genius of this nation. What we have already achieved gives us hope – the audacity to hope – for what we can and must achieve tomorrow."

Since dropping out in Iowa, Joe Biden had stayed behind the scenes, counseling Obama and Hillary Clinton in private on foreign policy matters. Not yet committed to either candidate, Biden called Obama's speech powerful, truthful and "one of the most important speeches we've heard in a long time. He told the story of America – both the good and the bad – and I believe his speech will come to represent an important step forward in race relations in our country."

Just a few hours later, Clinton spoke at Philadelphia City Hall. "Issues of race and gender in America have been complicated throughout our history, and they are complicated in this primary campaign. There have been detours and pitfalls along the way, but we should remember that this is a historic moment for the Democratic Party and for our country. We will be nominating the first African-American or woman for the presidency of the United States, and that is something that all Americans can and should celebrate."

Wright was no stranger to Wilmington and had preached at the Mother African Union Church, the first independent black church in the country. Months before the controversial clips aired nationwide, Wright came to August Quarterly, a celebration started by church founder Peter Spencer in 1814. Wright, then still leading his "unashamedly black and unapologetically Christian" congregation in Chicago, didn't give Obama much of a chance in the election. The candidate with the best message "doesn't win elections in America; money and connections do." Wright gave the early nod to Clinton.

Hours after Obama's speech on race, his opponent at the time, Hillary Clinton, spoke at Philadelphia City Hall: "Issues of race and gender in America have been complicated throughout our history, and they are complicated in this primary campaign ... but we should remember that this is a historic moment for the Democratic Party and for our country. We will be nominating the first African-American or woman for the presidency of the United States, and that is something that all Americans can and should celebrate."

HILLARYCLINTON.COM
READY TO
BRING OUR
TROOPS HOME

OBAMA
BIDEN
Military Families For Obama
Welcome Joe
OBAMA
BIDEN

Chapter 9: Greenville to Springfield

"Out of every bad thing that happens, if you search hard enough, you'll find something positive."

— Joe Biden, quoting his mother, Jean Finnegan Biden, hundreds of times over the years in campaign speeches, on television and to the man on the street

The Old Barley Mill was built along Brandywine Creek on land cultivated by Timen Stiddem, a Swede and passenger to the New World aboard the Kalmar Nyckel. A grist mill here dates to the 1640s. The barley mill to 1765. This is visceral Delaware. The Piedmont. The Wyeths.

Flour mills and the American Revolution, General Washington's battle at the Brandywine near Chadds Ford, gave way to gunpowder mills and the du Ponts, who bequeathed mansions such as Winterthur and a wellspring of roomy neighborhoods for Delaware's rich and powerful.

Here in Greenville, on Barley Mill Road, Joe Biden built his dream home.

Any given Saturday, Jill Biden might jog by. Joe, back from D.C. via Amtrak, might amble up to his mother's carriage house, situated at the top of a long driveway bisecting four acres, with pine and oak trees, a lake with a dock and a gorgeous 7,000-square-foot home.

On a hot day in August, insular and indomitable Greenville became the epicenter of a political parlor game called the Veepstakes.

Hillary Clinton, Obama's chief rival, was in the hunt. Evan Bayh, a moderate senator from Republican-leaning Indiana, and Gov. Tim Kaine of Virginia, a harbinger state for Southern tastes, were buzz-worthy. Kansas Gov. Kathleen Sebelius, who delivered the Democratic response to President Bush's State of the Union address, was intriguing but not an A-lister. Neither was Biden, the scrappy Irish kid from Scranton. Better suited for secretary of state, most pundits said, where his encyclopedic grasp of geopolitics could help Obama, a foreign policy novice, navigate strategic minefields in Iraq, Afghanistan, Pakistan, Russia and Georgia.

By the summer of 2008, the Obama campaign, led by Mill Creek, Del., native David Plouffe, had amassed 13 million people on its e-mail distribution list. Harnessing the energy of Facebook friending

Joe Biden leapt onto the stage in Springfield, Ill., in shirtsleeves after Obama introduced him as "the next vice president of the United States." Thousands crowded the grounds of the Old State Capitol, some standing on benches or garbage cans, many unable to see the stage through the sea of people.

and e-mail spam, Obama promised they'd "be the first to know" who he picked for vice president.

In early August, Caroline Kennedy and Eric Holder, who Obama later chose for attorney general, were vetting candidates. Obama said he'd reveal the name of the winner in a text message before a speech in Springfield, Ill., where Lincoln had given his famous "House Divided" speech in 1858, and his nominee would join him on stage on Aug. 23, a Saturday. The event would be a springboard to the Democratic National Convention, opening in Denver two days later.

The Springfield deadline scrambled the media. Reporters caught Bayh driving his twin sons to tennis camp, Kaine moving his son into college housing in Washington, D.C., and Biden swinging a golf club in Greenville while avoiding a mob of reporters tossing Frisbees, punching BlackBerrys and iPhones, and jockeying for a

For days, members of the local and national media camped out on the Bidens' Greenville lawn awaiting confirmation that the Delaware senator either was or was not Obama's choice as running mate. Every approaching car and "no comment" from a family member became fodder for new predictions. At right, the Hutt family from Newark, Del., (Michael, 8, mom Beth, dad Eric, Gideon, 3, and David, 1) joined a crowd outside the Greenville home after the announcement. They, as did dozens of others, wanted to catch a glimpse of Biden as he left for Springfield, Ill.

Congrats
Sen. Biden
Thanks for putting DE
on the map!!

high-rent patch of shade next to satellite trucks and TV vans.

On Tuesday, Aug. 19, a few reporters, a security guard and a pizza delivery man chatted outside Jean Biden's carriage house. Her son, unusually shy for the cameras, was curt when asked where he would be when Obama was in Springfield. "Here," said Biden. He ignored another question, flung from 20 yards. "You got better things to do, guys," he told reporters. "I'm not the guy."

For 24 hours, Biden's "I'm not the guy" coursed through cable's veins. Greenville calmed a bit, but Biden spokeswoman Elizabeth Alexander issued a curious clarification: Biden meant to say he didn't expect to be asked. By the next morning, Biden had relaxed. He delivered doughnuts, bagels and coffee to the crowd. He left his home before noon, telling reporters he was going to a landfill to dispose of tree branches. "I had a successful dump," Biden said when he returned about 90 minutes later. With the sun ablaze, a Biden staffer dropped off containers of lemon water ice.

On Thursday morning, the approach of a blue Buick LeSabre caused a stir. Like a school of fish, about a dozen journalists grabbed gear and leapt into position at the end of Biden's driveway. Biden, wearing a suit and sunglasses, nodded and waved from behind tinted windows before the car exited onto Barley Mill Road and disappeared. Most neighbors were amused by the microphones and cameras. "Elvis has left the building," one cameraman said after Biden's car rolled by.

Friday was epic. At 9:30 a.m., a woman who refused to identify her-

After days of anticipation, false leads and media scrutiny, Biden emerged from his family home as Obama's running mate. At right, in Springfield, with cell phone cameras clicking photos all around, the Obamas and Bidens acknowledged their supporters.

OBAMA.COM

AMTRAK
Gate C

self snapped pictures of the scene and drove away. New Castle County police showed up to roust reporters camped too close. Photographers chased a tip that a jet was waiting for Biden at the airport. One of Biden's staffers showed up, without stopping to chat. Three gardeners, mobbed in Biden's yard, said the lawn was healthy. As the evening wore on, Kaine and Bayh told friends they were out of the running.

More satellite trucks scrambled for Greenville. The blogosphere was frenetic.

At 3 a.m. East Coast time on Saturday, the text message was outbound: "Barack Obama has chosen Senator Joe Biden to be our VP nominee. Watch the first Obama-Biden rally live at 3 p.m. ET on www.BarackObama.com. Spread the word!"

By that bleary-eyed hour, the text was stale. Before midnight, old media broke the story online – Secret Service agents were protecting Biden. MSNBC, CNN and The Associated Press had it. Delawareonline posted the news on its Web site. The (Wilmington) News Journal went to print that night with Biden's name in headlines.

Four hours after the text, a half-dozen photographers were hunkered down at the entrance to the New Castle Airport. Newark residents Regina Betley and Bonnie Mucha, who had been at the airport Friday night, returned Saturday with handmade "Obama-Biden 2008" signs. When Biden's motorcade veered to a back entrance, a group hiked across the grass to peek through a fence. Biden's plane was on a distant runway.

Introduced as "the next vice president of the United States," Biden bounded onto the Springfield stage in shirtsleeves. Thousands gathered on the grounds of the Old State Capitol, some standing on benches or garbage cans. Most couldn't see a thing. For Delaware, Biden was nearing the highest office ever achieved by a First Stater – a legacy that included framers such as John Dickinson, Caesar Rodney and Gunning Bedford Jr., and legendary politicians such as William V. "Bill" Roth Jr. and William Wells.

The partnership seemed fitting: Obama, the upstart freshman senator, charmed the nation with his intellect and well-articulated ideals. Everyone talked about his potential, his promising future. Just like Delawareans had talked about young Joe Biden. In choosing him as vice president, Obama, a former political rival, placed Biden squarely on the national stage that for almost 40 years had eluded him. Biden's white hair was like a flag of experience as he worked the stage during a 15-minute speech, matching the length of Obama's remarks. Biden drew cheers and inspired chants of Obama's campaign slogan, "Yes, We Can."

"Ladies and gentlemen, these are no ordinary times, and this is no ordinary election," Biden said. "The truth of the matter is ... that the American Dream under four years, eight years of Bush and McCain, that American Dream is slipping away. I don't have to tell you that. You feel it in your lives. You see it in your shrinking wages. And the cost of everything from groceries to health care to college to filling up

Biden, who rode Amtrak to Washington for more than 35 years, greets porter Keith Lewis at the Wilmington station on Aug. 25, 2008. He boarded a train that began his journey to Denver and the Democratic National Convention.

your car at the gas station, it keeps going up and up and the future keeps receding further and further away as you reach for your dreams."

Although he was like family to First Staters, many in the Midwest were just getting to know Biden. Spectators held cell phones and cameras above their heads. Some held umbrellas to block the beating sun. Others wore floppy hats or baseball caps.

Obama called his running mate a "statesman with sound judgment" who has "stared down dictators" and a "man of fundamental decency" who has survived personal tragedy. Obama praised Biden's "fortitude" and "resilience" after he lost his wife and daughter in a car accident, and his ability to balance family and professional life.

Ebullient when he took the stage, Biden struck a serious tone, bemoaning the state of the economy and criticizing Republicans, including McCain, whom he called a friend. Biden said Obama's capabilities and the moment in history both lent themselves to the possibility of "literally changing the direction of the country and righting our place in the world. I don't have any problem being No. 2 and trying to help him do that because it is such an incredible moment. He obviously has the capacity to inspire. And he has the capacity, I think, to literally help the world look at us in a different way, a more positive way. So I'm excited to be a part of it."

About 850 miles due west of Greenville, Biden was right at home. "It's great to be here on the steps of the old Statehouse in the land of Lincoln. President Lincoln once instructed us – be sure to put your feet in the right place. Then, stand firm. Today, Springfield, I know my feet are in the right place."

To many residents of Delaware, Biden is simply "Joe." Two days after being tapped as Obama's running mate, he signed Mike Annone's construction helmet. At right, Jill Biden shows off her husband and Obama on the cover of Newsweek.

Cappuccino
PRESS
New Jersey
FABER
Books
Since 1848

Chapter 10: 'Hope and History'

"Let me end by saying this to you. You know I'm always quoting those Irish poets. But it is true, it is true, and I'll end this campaign the way I began it. History teaches us not to hope on this side of the grave. But then once in a lifetime now that longed-for tidal wave of justice rises up and hope and history rhyme. My prayer for you is, my plea to you is, make sure it does, make sure it does."

— Joe Biden in Des Moines, paraphrasing Seamus Heaney as he ended his run for the 2008 Democratic nomination

There's a shot of Joe Biden at a curbside barbecue stand in Denver, behind the counter, that toothy grin, arms around two African-American women in red "Boney's BBQ" T-shirts. They've paused for a photo op with this dude from Delaware, chip bags and styrofoam trays hanging in the background.

Beau Biden, dressed like Dad in navy blazer, khakis, Oxford open at the collar, is on the other side of the smokehouse counter. Delaware's Attorney General is probably holding the camera, taking this shot for the ladies. Hunter might be there. Other Bidens, but they melt away as Joe slips into character. "Hey. How ya doing?"

Biden orders pulled-pork sandwiches to go, grabs elbows and leans in as a crowd squeezes around him. Moms of soldiers in Iraq. A firefighter. Kids. When he talks, he nearly touches noses with a few. The barbecue arrives, he waves, walks to the waiting Secret Service motorcade at Denver's 16th Street Mall and is gone.

Part performance artist, part wiseguy, Biden was 48 hours away from cracking prime time – the slot he'd aimed for practically his entire life. A favorite on the Sunday morning news and late-night comedy hours, Biden rarely broke the logjam of candidates scheduled for "60 Minutes" or a live broadcast after supper, when most Americans tuned in. Bill and then Hillary Clinton. Obama. Gary Hart and Michael Dukakis. John Kerry and Al Gore upstaged and outspent him.

But folks on the street loved him, and when he finally arrived at the Pepsi Center for the Democratic National Convention to accept his party's

After two presidential tries and countless interviews out of the limelight, Joe Biden took center stage in prime time at the 2008 Democratic National Convention.

nomination it didn't matter anymore, he said, that the pinnacle was one notch below his dream.

On Aug. 27, 2008, the speeches were about him. The video was his life story.

As the hour approached, Biden stood offstage, listening to his oldest son.

Beau talked about the accident that killed his mother Neilia and sister Naomi. He talked about his father's childhood stutter and his father's long trips from D.C. to Wilmington to catch his sons' ball games or his granddaughter's birthday party.

Michelle Obama, sitting in the audience, wiped tears from her cheeks.

"As a single parent, he decided to be there to put us to bed, to be there when we woke from a bad dream, to make us breakfast, so he'd travel to and from Washington, four hours a day," Beau said. "Five years later, he married my mom, Jill. They together rebuilt our family. And 36 years later, he still makes that trip. So even though Dad worked in Washington, he's never been part of Washington. He always sounded like the kid from Scranton, Pennsylvania, he is. And even that is a story of overcoming."

After the car wreck, the aneurysms, two failed bids for the presidency, gaffes about Delaware's slave state history and Indian accents at Dunkin' Donuts, Biden clawed his way back. One of his most endearing qualities – his gift for gab – was also one of the most damning. His speech at the Democratic National Convention would be the first hard test of his ability to safely articulate Obama's vision to those coveted middle-class Americans. He could dazzle and diss anyone in a debate on the issues. He could charm a taxi driver or a coffee barista, one on one, but his appeal in the national spotlight, on stage alone, was untested.

Political patsies for eight years, Democrats had hope and a gut full of doubt. Hillary Clinton, a link to Democratic heydays, interrupted the night's delegate roll call to move the historic nomination of the first African-American atop a major party presidential

First a video told Joe Biden's life story. Then Beau came on stage and spoke about his father, the accident, the nightly trips home to put his sons to bed. "Be there for my dad like he was for me. Be there for Barack Obama because our country needs him." After the introduction, the crowd exploded and father and son hugged.

BIDEN

ticket. The long, hard primary tested and strengthened Obama, President Clinton had said earlier. "And in his first presidential decision, the selection of a running mate, he hit it out of the park. With Joe Biden's experience and wisdom, supporting Barack Obama's proven understanding, instincts and insight, America will have the national security leadership we need."

As Denver approached, middle-class voters were inching toward presumptive Republican presidential candidate John McCain. A Gallup poll conducted Aug. 18-24 showed conservative Democrats moving away from Obama. On Aug. 26, Gallup's daily tracking poll put McCain (46 percent) ahead of Obama (44 percent) for the first time all summer.

A day later, Biden was waiting for his son to introduce him.

"Be there for my dad like he was for me. Be there for Barack Obama because our country needs him. Be there for both of them because millions of families need to know that their best days aren't behind them, but ahead of them. Be there for both of them because millions of people are trying to overcome, just like my dad overcame. Be there. Be there because Barack Obama and Joe Biden will deliver America the change we so desperately need. Please join me in welcoming my friend, my father, my hero and the next vice president of the United States: Joe Biden."

The Pepsi Center erupted.

In a royal blue tie, Biden walked out and hugged Beau, who kissed him on the cheek and flicked something off his shoulder. The two walked to the edge of the stage to greet Sen. John Kerry and House Speaker Nancy Pelosi. Biden put an arm around his son, and poked a finger at faces in the crowd, guiding Beau around like a kid in the St. Patrick's Day parade.

It was 10:30 p.m. in Delaware.

"God, I wish my dad was here tonight, but I thank God and am so grateful that my mom, Catherine Eugenia Finnegan Biden, is here tonight. Mom, I love you," Biden said. "You know, my mom taught her children – all the children who flocked to our house – that you are defined by your sense of honor, and you are redeemed by your loyalty. She believes bravery lives in every heart and her expectation is that it will be summoned. Failure. Failure at some point in your life is inevitable, but giving up is unforgivable."

It was not a slam dunk speech. When he raised his voice, a chord perfected for pipefitters and cops, he strained. But he touched all the right themes – the danger of Bush and Cheney. McCain's record of voting with Bush 95 percent of the time. Family. Biden was hoeing for common soil.

"Almost every single night, I take the train home to Wilmington, Delaware, sometimes very late. As I sit there in my seat and I look out that window, I see those flickering lights of the homes that pass by, I can almost hear the conversation they're having at the kitchen table after they put their kids to bed. Like millions of Americans, they're asking questions as ordinary as they are profound. Questions they never, ever thought they'd have to ask themselves."

Should mom move in with us now that dad is gone? Fifty, sixty, seven-

Biden's convention speech touched on familiar themes – middle-class values, family, attacks on the Bush administration. It was solid and on-point throughout with one inspired ad-lib that brought down the house.

ty dollars to fill up the car? Winter's coming. How we gonna pay the heating bills? Another year and no raise? Did you hear the company may be cutting our health care? Now, we owe more on the house than it's worth. How are we going to send the kids to college? How are we gonna be able to retire?

"That's the America that George Bush has left us, and that's the America [we] will continue to get if George, excuse me, if John McCain is elected president of the United States of America. Freudian slip. Freudian slip."

It was Biden's best line, ad-libbed. The delegates loved it.

"Folks, these are not isolated discussions among families down on their luck. These are common stories among middle-class people who've worked hard their whole life, played by the rules on the promise that their tomorrows would be better than their yesterdays. That promise is the promise of America. It defines who we are as a people. And now, and now it's in jeopardy. I know it. You know it. But John McCain doesn't seem to get it. Barack Obama gets it, though. Like many of us in this room, like many of us in this hall, Barack Obama has worked his way up. His is a great American story."

This was the Biden of Scranton and Claymont. The kid from the coal town.

"Jill and I are truly honored to join Michelle and Barack on this journey. When I look at their young children – and when I look at my grandchildren – I know why I'm here. I'm here for their future. I am here for everyone I grew up with in Scranton and Wilmington. I am here for the cops and firefighters, the teachers and assembly line workers – the folks whose lives are the very measure of whether the American dream endures."

He ended and gave a short wave. He drifted to his left, and then right, pointing. He drank in the cheers, but seemed tired. In the span of a week, his life shifted from the downside slide of a senior senator to the uphill climb of historic presidential aspirations. Jill joined him for a hug, clutching a microphone. "And honey, tonight we have a very special surprise guest," she said.

"Who?" Joe replied.

Screams met Obama's first convention appearance.

"Hello, Democrats. I just wanted to come out here for a little, little something to say. I want everybody to know, understand why I am so proud to have Joe Biden and Jill Biden and Beau Biden and Mama Biden and the whole Biden family with me on this journey to take America back."

Bidens from all corners drifted in. Frankie. Hunter. Finnegan. Jimmie. Ashley. Too many to count. Joe leaned down and embraced his mother. At the front of the stage, his grandkids waved furiously at delegates in the crowd shaking placards and name posts. Biden bent over beside them.

The next night, at Invesco Field at Mile High, Obama accepted the nomination of the Democratic party.

Election Day was 68 days away.

On the last night of the convention, Obama accepted the Democratic party's presidential nomination before more than 70,000 at Invesco Field.

SCHOOL
SUNDAES

Chapter 11: Vs. Palin

"The most dangerous vice president we've had probably in American history."

— Joe Biden's assessment of Vice President Dick Cheney during his Oct. 2, 2008, debate with Gov. Sarah Palin at Washington University in St. Louis.

Two days before his debate with Sarah Palin, Joe Biden took Beau's family to lunch at the Charcoal Pit, a roadside diner with ketchup on the table and a jukebox with CDs in every booth. Beau's wife Hallie and daughter Natalie sat down. Beau ordered a cheesesteak and a black and white milkshake for Dad, fries and burgers. Biden worked the room and shared a moment with Bert Boyle, who'd worked the cash register at the Concord Pike "Pit" since Biden was a football star at Archmere Academy some 50 years ago. He cradled her face in his hands.

Palin and Biden had been holed up in "debate prep" for days, Palin at John McCain's Arizona ranch with his senior advisers, Biden in Wilmington, sparring with Michigan Gov. Jennifer Granholm. But Biden couldn't resist the tug of an old haunt.

The vice presidential debate was the most anticipated in history, and a stumble by either candidate would be live bait for 70 million viewers. For all of the unpredictable quotes – calling Bush brain dead, Obama clean and articulate – Biden is at his core a predictable creature: the boy calming a stutter by reciting poetry in the mirror. His childhood trips to Scranton didn't stop when he became a senator. Those same Irish poets – Heaney and Yeats – filled his speeches on the campaign trail.

In an interview for *The New Yorker* in 2005 about the politics of national security, Biden couldn't resist an anecdote about his homespun habits with writer Jeffrey Goldberg.

" 'That night, I got off that trip, from Scranton, I got off the plane, Wilmington airport, only private aircraft, get off, pick up a phone, call a local place called the Charcoal Pit before it closes. They have great steak sandwiches and a milkshake. Triple-thick milkshake. And I hadn't eaten. I'm going to pass it on the way home. They're literally sweeping the floors. A woman, overweight, forty years old, a little unkempt, had a tooth missing in the side, not in the front' – he showed his flashing white teeth, to demonstrate – 'walks up to me to give me my steak sandwich.' "

Joe Biden is a well-known figure at the Charcoal Pit. "They have great steak sandwiches." He took time out from preparations for the vice presidential debate with Sarah Palin to lunch with son Beau, his wife Hallie and their daughter Natalie.

VISA

When Biden walked into the Charcoal Pit on Sept. 30, 2008, he had something on his mind other than the Palin debate. At the end of the week, Beau's National Guard unit would fly to Texas before deployment in Iraq. The lunch chat was like hundreds at Grandpop Finnegan's, where Biden's uncles argued politics over a few drinks. Young "Joey" absorbed those kitchen table lessons, among them the dangers of alcohol.

"Debates are important but family is always what's really important," Biden spokesman David Wade told reporters squeezing into the diner. "The Biden family, like all the families in our country who have a loved one called up, deserve some time to themselves outside the glare and frenzy of the political process."

Less than 24 hours before he was to meet Palin at Washington University in St. Louis, Biden broke from preparations to travel to the Capitol to vote on the controversial $700 billion plan to bail out Wall Street. Holding a cup of coffee and talking on his cell phone, Biden boarded the train around 6:30 p.m., with Secret Service agents at his side. Later, he made a brief public appearance, walking to the dining car to shake hands and chat. The bailout passed by a wide margin, 74-25, with Biden, McCain and Obama both voting in favor.

Biden hopped the 10 p.m. train to Wilmington and then took a chartered 737 to St. Louis, arriving a few hours before PBS senior correspondent Gwen Ifill led off the night. Palin opened by asking Biden if she could call him "Joe," and the two settled into a fairly tame 90 minutes of he-said, she-said. Biden ruled the substantive discussions on the banking crisis, Pakistan and the role of a vice president under the U.S. Constitution. Palin stuck to a narrow script of defending McCain, blaming Washington and reaching out to regular folks.

"One thing that Americans do at this time, also, though, is let's commit ourselves to just everyday American people, Joe Six Pack, hockey moms across the nation, I think we need to band together and say never again. Never will we be exploited and taken advantage of again by those who are managing our money and loaning us these dollars."

A Washington University instant poll of undecided voters said Palin was more likable and voters favored her folksy style over Biden's scholarly approach, but gave the edge to Biden when it came to his grasp of the issues. Palin used the word "maverick" to describe McCain six times before Biden countered with his best punch.

"Look, the maverick – let's talk about the maverick John McCain is. And, again, I love him. He's been a maverick on some issues, but he has been no maverick on the things that matter to people's lives. He voted four out of five times for George Bush's budget, which put us a half a trillion dollars in debt this year and over $3 trillion in debt since he's got there. He has not been a maverick in providing health care for people. He has voted against ... including another 3.6

Bert Boyle waited on Biden at the "Pit" when he was a high school football star.

As they greeted each other before the debate, Sarah Palin asked Biden if she could call him "Joe." By most accounts, the Biden-Palin debate was a draw. One poll said Palin was more likable but Biden had a better grasp of the issues.

THE UNION AND THE CONSTITUTION FOREVER.

million children in coverage of the existing health care plan, when he voted in the United States Senate. He's not been a maverick when it comes to education. He has not supported tax cuts and significant changes for people being able to send their kids to college. He's not been a maverick on the war. He's not been a maverick on virtually anything that genuinely affects the things that people really talk about around their kitchen table."

After a disastrous series of national interviews, Palin rebounded in St. Louis. McCain had gambled on Palin's appeal to homemakers in Ohio and soccer moms in Florida. "She is exactly who this country needs to help us fight the same old Washington politics of me first and country second," said McCain, who flew to Dayton, Ohio, to announce the surprise selection. Days after the Republican National Convention in St. Paul ended on Sept. 4, 60 percent of those polled by USA Today/Gallup rated McCain's choice of Palin excellent or pretty good.

But then Palin sat down with Katie Couric. Biden's missteps played out in the media like old comfortable shoes, Palin's hit like missiles. On Sept. 25, CBS aired its exclusive interview.

Couric: "Explain to me why [Alaska's proximity to Russia] enhances your foreign policy credentials."

The week after the debate, self-described hockey mom Sarah Palin, with her family beside her, threw out the puck at the Philadelphia Flyers season opener.

Palin: "Well, it certainly does because our – our next-door neighbors are foreign countries, there in the state that I am the executive of."

Couric: "Have you ever been involved with any negotiations, for example, with the Russians?"

Palin: "We have trade missions back and forth. We, we do. It's very important when you consider even national security issues with Russia as [Prime Minister Vladimir] Putin rears his head and comes into the airspace of the United States of America. Where, where do they go? It's Alaska. It's just right over the border. It is from Alaska that we send those out to make sure that an eye is being kept on this very powerful nation, Russia, because they are right there. They are right next to, to our state."

Two nights later, "Saturday Night Live" aired a parody of the interview with Tina Fey as Palin and Amy Poehler as Couric. The SNL segment was poisonously close to the real thing. By Oct. 31-Nov. 2, only 35 percent of those polled by USA Today/Gallup said McCain's choice of Palin was excellent or pretty good.

Biden and Palin spent the last weeks of the campaign crisscrossing the country – Palin to huge crowds, Biden to small gatherings. When Palin came to the Wachovia Center to drop the first puck at the Philadelphia Flyers season opener, some fans booed.

At the end of October, a television ad aired with audio of Biden's remarks at a Seattle fundraiser. "Watch, we're going to have an international crisis, a generated crisis to test the mettle of this guy," Biden told the small, private gathering. By then, Biden was using a teleprompter at rallies and no longer took questions from the crowd. He insisted he wasn't "muzzled" by a nervous Obama campaign, but Biden, who doesn't drink, couldn't resist the compulsion to confide.

The night before Halloween, Biden and Palin nearly ran into each other in Williamsport, Pa., where Little League baseball was born almost 70 years before. Election Day was just five days away.

The former lumber capital of the world, Williamsport once was home to scores of millionaires, who built majestic Victorian mansions along Fourth Street, known by residents as "Millionaires Row." By 2008, jobs were scarce. A public housing complex was built two blocks away from Millionaires Row.

In a baseball stadium, Palin addressed a lively crowd estimated at 10,000. "Folks, the far left wing of the Democratic Party is getting ready to take over government." One woman wore a rubber Hillary Clinton mask; one man proudly waved a sign: "Gun Slingin' Bible Clingin' Redneck."

Biden's streamlined message was brief and on point, a script he'd mostly followed since the debate. The indoor rally at Lycoming College was small by design. "The question in this election is not are you better off today than you were four years ago. We're beyond that. ... The question is, who is going to make us better off four years from now?"

Biden interrupted preparations for his vice presidential debate with Sarah Palin to vote for the $700 billion Wall Street bailout in the Senate. He arrived back in Wilmington late at night, but took time out to talk with Amtrak employee Jeff Clinger, one of dozens of Joe's friends who work at the train station.

VOTING ON DELAWARE'S ELECTRONIC VOTING MACHINE

Chapter 12: Election Day

"Patience had never been my strength, but somewhere in that second hospital stay I had started to think about the virtue of being in less of a hurry. ... The presidency, for instance, could wait. There would be another time if I really wanted it. The restoration of my reputation would be a long process. Time would tell."

— Joe Biden in "Promises to Keep"

On an unseasonably mild November night in downtown Chicago, thousands filled the grounds of Grant Park. Jesse Jackson and Oprah Winfrey, squeezed into the crowd, could be seen crying. Flags waved and spotlights roamed the night sky, filling in the blanks of the city's lights. The crowd's roars could be heard blocks away as returns were reported on Jumbotrons, showing Barack Obama winning the key states of Pennsylvania, Ohio and Iowa.

There would be no hanging chads or Supreme Court opinions. On Nov. 4, 2008, Obama redrew the electoral map, closing the deal in Ohio and Florida. Obama took 365 electoral votes, McCain 173. With 69 million individual votes, to McCain's 60 million, Obama won a share of the popular vote larger than any Democrat had since Lyndon Johnson in 1964.

Delaware's garrulous, amiable and seemingly ever-present Joe Biden was introduced to the world as vice president-elect of the United States of America, an unplanned chapter in his legacy as a career politician. He wasn't a celebrity in the campaign – not like Obama or Sarah Palin, relative newcomers to U.S. politics. But he was a known quantity, a man the pundits and the media called "experienced" and "accomplished" and "comfortable on the world stage." He was "steady" and "safe," a man who had been through personal tragedy and survived.

At Obama's side, Biden and his family took the stage in a city more than three times as large as the state of Delaware. At midnight Eastern time, Obama addressed the Grant Park crowd.

"If there is anyone out there who still doubts that America is a place where all things are possible; who still wonders if the dream of

Just after 9 a.m. on Election Day, Joe Biden cast his ballot with Jill, daughter Ashley and mother Jean. Aside from his thumbs-up, he offered little comment, save a light-hearted warning to his mother: "Don't tell them who you voted for, now."

our founders is alive in our time; who still questions the power of our democracy, tonight is your answer. ... It's the answer spoken by young and old, rich and poor, Democrat and Republican, black, white, Latino, Asian, Native American, gay, straight, disabled and not disabled – Americans who sent a message to the world that we have never been a collection of red states and blue states: We are, and always will be, the United States of America."

There's only one way it could have been better for Biden, but that story's already been told. This was the start of a new chapter. Biden, who had been his own boss for decades, had for nine weeks been trying out the role of No. 2, making whirlwind campaign stops to win voters to the Democratic ticket. Since he was announced as Obama's pick, he had led close to 90 rallies and fundraisers, crisscrossing the country, stopping at hamburger joints and ice cream shops, college gymnasiums and retirement villages. He visited at least 20 states – from Colorado to Iowa, Missouri to Montana, Pennsylvania to Indiana.

An estimated 70 million Americans watched Biden and Palin debate on Oct. 3, and he'd done more than 200 interviews with the media. On election day, Biden trudged the final steps toward victory, starting his day in Delaware just after 9 a.m., when he cast his ballot with his wife and daughter and mom. Throngs of supporters gathered outside Tatnall School near Biden's Greenville home to get a glimpse of the hometown candidate. Many held "Delaware for Biden" signs above their heads and chanted Biden's name.

Another group, holding a McCain for President sign, shouted "Sarah, Sarah," in support of Palin. Biden gave a thumbs-up as he exited the polling booth, but said little at the start of the long day that took him first to Richmond, Va., then Chicago for the finale of the long campaign.

"All right, Mom," Biden said, taking his mother's hand after casting his ballot. "Don't tell them who you voted for, now."

The family had been out late the night before. The Bidens drew a crowd of about 2,000 in Philadelphia late Nov. 3, with Jimmy Rollins, shortstop of the 2008 World Series champion Philadelphia Phillies, introducing them. It was the last of scores of rallies for Biden, who gave a mixture of canned pep talks and spontaneous remarks throughout the 2008 campaign, sounding familiar themes – over and over and over again: Restore the middle class. Reach across the congressional aisle. End the war. Reclaim America's respect in the world.

"One of the highlights is the degree of the enthusiasm," Biden said on Election Day during a short interview aboard his chartered 737. "The energy is just amazing. It's just amazing."

Ironically, Biden was the quiet candidate. Known for more than three decades for being long-winded and outspoken, he had taken a back seat. His campaign stops and speeches often flew underneath the radar of the national media. Palin got a story practically every

Crowds gathered outside Tatnall School to get a glimpse of Biden as he voted. "One of the highlights is the degree of the enthusiasm," Biden said.

BAPTISTS FOR
OBAMA
OBAMA OBAMA

time she changed clothes; Biden usually got a headline only when he stuck his foot in his mouth.

Most of his gaffes during the vice presidential run were harmless, if embarrassing. "Stand up, Chuck, let 'em see ya!" he famously shouted to a public official using a wheelchair in Columbia, Mo. Later, he told a crowd in Nashua, N.H., that Hillary Clinton "might have been a better pick than me" for vice president, causing a minor stir. And during an interview with CBS's Katie Couric, he got some historical facts mixed up, saying, "When the stock market crashed, Franklin D. Roosevelt got on the television and didn't just talk about the, you know, the princes of greed." FDR wasn't president during the stock market crash of 1929, and televisions weren't commonplace.

Biden dismisses the notion that any of his verbal missteps negatively affected the campaign, though McCain used Biden's own words against him more than once. "It's been nasty," Biden said on the flight to Chicago, the election still in doubt. "I feel badly because they've reserved all their nastiness for Barack. You know, he's been the brunt of it. I tell you what, he's tough. The guy is unflappable."

Comedians picked up on some of Biden's flubs, though only late in the campaign – after Tina Fey put on lipstick and a snappy suit to mimic Sarah Palin on "Saturday Night Live." Near the end of the campaign, SNL's Jason Sudeikis donned a silver wig and a 100-watt smile to channel Biden in a sketch, a parody of a C-SPAN segment called "Joe Biden and John Murtha Say Crazy Things in Johnstown, Pa."

Thousands gathered in Grant Park in Chicago on election night, and as the results rolled in, roars could be heard blocks away. At midnight Eastern time, Obama addressed the crowd, making a point to acknowledge what his running mate brought to the campaign.

Murtha, a senator from Pennsylvania, gained unflattering press after saying his home turf is racist.

In the skit, Sudeikis, aka Biden, says: " ... remember this: If Barack Obama is elected, we will have a crisis. And when this crisis hits, and it will, in the second week of February, we may do some weird things. We may cede Florida back to Spain, or Alaska to the Russians. We may blow up every nuclear power plant in the country ..."

Biden, who watched the skits on the Web, said he wasn't offended. "I think that's good stuff. It's not nasty. It's funny. I mean, compared to what they're doing with others, hey, man." Biden laughed. "I feel blessed."

Almost three dozen Biden family members and friends, who filled the front 15 or so rows of the plane, applauded when Biden boarded in Wilmington on Election Day. Among them: Jill, and all four of her sisters and their families, his mother Jean, daughter Ashley, sister Valerie, brother Jim, son Hunter and his family. Also aboard was Biden's longtime political adviser, Ted Kaufman, who later took Biden's seat in the Senate, and about 12 staff members. Beau was not aboard. A member of the Delaware National Guard, he was with his unit in Texas preparing to go to Iraq. Though commanders agreed to release him for Election Night, "he won't do it," Biden said.

During the flight, Biden took off his suit jacket and strode the aisle at the front of the plane, chatting with family, once venturing to the back of the plane to visit briefly with the media. Win or lose, it would all be over in a few hours' time. Late that morning, there was time for just one last stop – at a Richmond polling place. One voter there hugged Biden so hard, her hat fell off.

Biden spent about 20 minutes shaking hands and signing autographs for the small crowd of mostly black voters gathered outside in a cold drizzle. He held a toddler in a pink winter coat, posing for a photograph. He leaned into a Nissan Altima to visit with a first-time voter. "There are a hundred moments like that," Biden said. Along a rope line in Colorado, a man had given him a Gold Star, which signifies the loss of a service member in war. "He wanted me to have it because he wanted us to end this war. This guy lost his son."

Not long before arriving in Chicago, Biden's granddaughter Finnegan held an impromptu news conference in the back of the plane, stopping to chat with reporters while on her way to the bathroom. She was 10 on election night. Fiddling with her necklace, her long blond hair pulled back in a ponytail, she contemplated another sleepover with the Obama girls. In his campaign speeches, Biden often mentioned how his granddaughters and Obama's two daughters had a pajama party during the Democratic National Convention in Denver.

"Did you tell them anything nice?" Biden asked playfully when he came to check on her after a few minutes. He hugged her. "I subscribe to anything Finnegan says. She's the one who pushed the hardest for me to run for vice president."

After Obama gave his victory speech, Biden's family joined the crowd on stage. Biden's mother held the hands of her son and Obama as they walked her to the front of the stage to wave to the crowd. ***Overleaf:*** *Just after midnight on Election Night, Obama took the stage in Chicago's Grant Park and captivated supporters: "If there is anyone out there who still doubts that America is a place where all things are possible; who still wonders if the dream of our founders is alive in our time; who still questions the power of our democracy, tonight is your answer. ... It's the answer spoken by young and old, rich and poor, Democrat and Republican, black, white, Latino, Asian, Native American, gay, straight, disabled and not disabled – Americans who sent a message to the world that we have never been a collection of red states and blue states: We are, and always will be, the United States of America."*

In Chicago, Biden spent the afternoon doing interviews via satellite television. He planned to watch election returns with Obama and his family. Hours before the polls closed, Biden contemplated a loss. "If we lose, look, the way I've always viewed every election, it will be fine if we lose. I mean, I'll be fine. ... If we lost the presidential and we lost the Senate race, well, then, you know, it means it's time for me to move on to something else. I don't expect that to happen. ... But I genuinely, I don't have any problem accepting the verdict of the American people and the people of Delaware. None. None at all."

Biden's family joined him on stage in Chicago after Obama gave his victory speech. A beaming Jill, wearing a sage green suit, strode onto the stage to hug her husband. Biden's mother Jean held the hands of her son and Obama as they walked her to the front of the stage to wave to the crowd. Biden's children came out, and his grandchildren, a big happy family. Biden lifted Finnegan in the air, holding her up to the crowd, smiling.

Biden had played a pivotal role in the Democrats' win, pundits said, enjoying higher approval ratings as voters got to know him and a ringing endorsement from Colin Powell, a Republican former secretary of state and chairman of the Joint Chiefs of Staff. Powell said Obama picked a running mate who is "ready to be president on day one."

During his victory speech, Obama acknowledged his running mate.

"I want to thank my partner in this journey, a man who campaigned from his heart, and spoke for the men and women he grew up with on the streets of Scranton and rode with on the train home to Delaware, the vice president-elect of the United States, Joe Biden."

Delaware Joe finally found his way to the White House, or as close as anyone can get short of winning the presidency.

During the victory speech in Grant Park, cameras found many in the crowd crying, including Oprah Winfrey and the Rev. Jesse Jackson.

TON
RENEWING AMERICA'S
2009
PROMISE

Chapter 13: Whistle-stop

"So to the people of Delaware, who have given me the honor of serving them, there's no way I can ever, ever express to them how much it's meant to me."

— Joe Biden in his farewell speech to the Senate on Jan. 15, 2009

Claymont, a steel town and bedroom community, is the "place where Joe Biden grew up."

But for most of the 2008 presidential campaign, Biden's first Delaware home was ignored while national media trudged through the other place Joe grew up – Scranton. But on a bitterly cold Saturday in mid-January, Claymont waited for its moment – a train from the north, slowing down to pass by the Amtrak station.

The train never stopped in Claymont, but images of Barack Obama, smiling and waving as he passed by, were captured for the ages.

Hundreds gathered at the northern Delaware station to see Obama's re-creation of Abraham Lincoln's whistle-stop trip to Washington before his 1861 inaugural. In three days, Obama would become the nation's first African-American president. In a few moments, he would stop in Wilmington to pick up Biden, his vice president.

People came from all over. Jerome Bowers walked down the hill from his home. Tara Anderson and Laurel Kirby came from California. Newark's Dena Brown pushed her daughter Jennifer's wheelchair. "We wanted to be part of history, too."

As the train neared the Claymont station, parents held their children up for a better view, motorists pulled onto the shoulder to watch. Obama and wife Michelle waved from a platform on the back of the train. A woman in the crowd hugged people near her, walked back to her car and cried.

Tens of thousands lined the tracks along the whistle-stop route – which started in Philadelphia and stopped in Wilmington and Baltimore before delivering the president and vice president to Washington.

Obama echoed Lincoln in speeches, delivered along, above and below the Mason-Dixon Line. In Philadelphia and again in

The Obamas and Bidens wave to the crowd at the Wilmington station as the pre-inaugural whistle-stop train departs for Baltimore. The trip from Philadelphia to Washington was one of many homages to Abraham Lincoln.

RENEWING AMERICA'S
PROMISE
Don't miss the train!
Carpool to
Statio
Save money,
time
and space
DART
1-888-RIDE-MATCH
ridesharedelaware.org

Baltimore, he said "that a government of, by, and for the people can endure" and made "an appeal not to our easy instincts but to our better angels."

"Together, we know that America faces its own crossroads – a nation at war, an economy in turmoil, an American Dream that feels like it's slipping away," Obama said to nearly 8,000 people at Wilmington's Tubman-Garrett Riverfront Park. "Together, we know that the American people are facing adversity, and that the time has come to pick ourselves up once again."

To hear those speeches first-hand required enduring long waits and temperatures in the teens. Some people passed out or simply couldn't outlast the bitter cold. Though Lincoln gave about 100 speeches during his circuitous 12-day train ride to Washington, he never made it to Wilmington.

Hearing of an assassination plot in Maryland, he reportedly disguised himself and hustled through the night from Philadelphia to Washington.

Wilmington promised to give Obama a much warmer welcome. Thousands had turned out for his February 2008 campaign stop in Rodney Square, and voters here backed him by a nearly 2-1 ratio in November. Tubman-Garrett had been chosen for its proximity to the Wilmington train station and for its symbolism. Harriet Tubman, a former slave, led hundreds of slaves along the Underground Railroad, which ran through Delaware, and Thomas Garrett offered his home in Wilmington's Quaker Hill neighborhood as a refuge for escaping slaves.

Before dawn that Saturday, Tubman-Garrett began filling with people. Vendors hawked buttons, flags, shirts, anything with Obama's name and face on it.

The crowd pressed as close as a temporary steel gate and the Secret Service would let them. Some climbed trees to get a better vantage point. By 10 a.m., the whistle-stop tour officially began in Philadelphia's 30th Street Station.

"We are here to mark the beginning of our journey to Washington," Obama told the crowd. "This is fitting because it was here, in this city, that our American journey began. It was here that a group of farmers and lawyers, merchants and soldiers gathered to declare their independence and lay claim to a destiny that they were being denied."

Obama and his wife, Michelle, boarded the shiny blue Georgia 300 rail car, coupled to an Amtrak engine, for the daylong trip south. The Pullman car, built in 1930, features painted walls, cherry wood and brass Pullman lamps, as well as a host of modern amenities. It's the same one he used in April 2008 on a whistle-stop tour from Philadelphia to Harrisburg.

As the train pulled into the Wilmington station, 13-year-old Nicodemus Williams wowed the crowd with a solo performance of "The Star-Spangled Banner." A student at Cab Calloway School of the Arts in Wilmington, Williams got word a day before that he would be singing at the event. "I was in total disbelief, total shock," he said.

In Claymont, Obama's train slowed to a crawl for the hundreds who had waited hours in subfreezing temperatures to see the president-elect, if only for a moment.

The crowd swelled to 7,875. Flags and stars-and-stripes bunting decorated the stage, and thousands of people waved small American flags. Upbeat music and snippets of Obama's speeches played over the loudspeakers, keeping the crowd entertained during the wait. A few times, they entertained themselves by singing "America the Beautiful."

First on the stage was Amtrak conductor Gregg Weaver, who regularly took Biden on his daily commute to Washington. He introduced Biden as "Amtrak's No. 1 commuter." Biden joked that he would sometimes have the train held for him when he was running late. "I'd be coming down Martin Luther King Boulevard. I'd call in here to Ron [Edwards, station manager] and say 'Ron, I can see the light. I'm only two away. What do you think?' And he'd say, 'I'll check with Gregg.' There was always some mechanical difficulty that prevented it from leaving."

Biden thanked Delaware for supporting him for the past 36 years and for helping to propel him to the vice presidency. He rephrased a line from James Joyce: "When I die, Delaware will be written on my heart."

At 12:51 p.m., Obama took the stage with his wife. After the cheering subsided, the crowd broke into "Happy Birthday" for Michelle Obama, who was turning 45. Obama spent almost half of his speech praising Biden's 36 years of public service. "Joe has always fought for the middle class, while forging the consensus to get things done. He

Above, members of UAW Local 1183 in Newark offered a suggestion for the new president's stimulus plan during the whistle-stop. At right, Biden addressed the crowd outside the train station he had used almost daily for more than 36 years.

RENEWING
AMERICA'S
PROMISE
WWW.PIC2009.ORG

has supported the cops and firefighters and families who form the backbone of our communities, while emerging as a statesman in the community of nations. Now, Delaware, I'm asking Joe Biden to take one more ride to Washington."

Obama then highlighted several people he had met on the campaign trail.

"Those are the stories that we will carry with us to Washington."

One of those was the story of Quincy Lucas, a Dover teacher whose sister died in a domestic violence incident. She shared the train ride with Obama and Biden. "These are the quiet heroes who have made this country great.

They work hard, they look after their families, they sacrifice for their children and their grandchildren, and they deserve a government that represents the same enduring values that they live out in their own lives."

Obama wrapped up his short speech by appealing to Delawareans' pride. "It was here, in Delaware, that the Constitution was first ratified. It was here, in Delaware, where the First State joined our union. Now it falls to us to carry forward that American story, and to make it our own." Obama spent 10 minutes shaking as many hands as he could reach before boarding the Pullman car at the rear of the train. Michelle Obama pulled the whistle this time. "See you at the next stop," Obama yelled.

The Wilmington crowd lingered a little longer, posing for pictures and hitting the portable bathrooms.

Eyerce Postom of Hockessin had come with her sister, Vondra Armstrong, of Little Rock, Ark. Armstrong made the trip just to see Obama in Wilmington and would head to D.C. for the inauguration. Even though they had been standing in the cold since 6 a.m., they remained ebullient as Obama's train pulled away.

"It's cold, my feet hurt, but we endured," Postom said. "It was awesome." On the train, the Obamas and Bidens chatted and joked with their fellow travelers.

The topic turned to Obama's inauguration speech, and Michelle Obama said she thought it was going to be good.

"That's not what you're supposed to say in front of the press," Obama said, aware that expectations are high for the event. "You're supposed to say it's gonna be all right."

The train slowed as it approached Edgewood Station in Edgewood, Md., where the crowd chanted "Obama!"

About 3:30 p.m., the train arrived at Baltimore's War Memorial Plaza, where Obama repeated much of the speech he had given in Philadelphia. He ended with the same call to action he delivered on election night.

"Let's make sure this election is not the end of what we do to change America, but the beginning. Join me in this effort. Join one another in this effort. And together, mindful of our proud history, hopeful for the future, let's seek a better world in our time."

At Tubman-Garrett Riverfront Park, just across from the Wilmington train station, Obama rallied the crowd and told them the story of Quincy Lucas, of Dover, whose sister was killed in a domestic violence incident.

Epilogue: Super Joe

"If you do politics the right way, you can actually make people's lives better. And integrity is the minimum ante to get into the game."

— Joe Biden in "Promises to Keep"

Call them Close Encounters of the Joe kind. At the Amtrak station, a hog pen at the state fair, eating a cheeseburger at the Charcoal Pit, standing in line for a movie at the Brandywine Town Center. Maybe picking up coffee at Brew HaHa! in Trolley Square. Maybe at Mass at St. Joseph on the Brandywine.

Joe's got a story for everyone, and everybody's got a story about Joe.

In pursuit of justice – on foot

On Nov. 20, 1977, I was nearing my house at 28th and North Broom streets, walking with my hands full, and a very fast kid came running, snatched my purse off my arm, and booked down Broom Street. Sen. Joe Biden was driving by my house, saw me running, heard my screams and saw this boy running with a purse, headed east on 27th Street. Biden headed his car down 27th Street, jumped out of the car – not thinking, "Gee, I'm a senator. Let the cops do this." – ran through a couple of backyards, over a couple of fences, and was gaining on this kid, when the kid threw down the pocketbook and continued to run. Biden retrieved my purse, and brought it back to me. For 30 years, I have kept this pocketbook. I wrote him ... and told him I was keeping it so that, one day, if he became president, he would sign it for me. He said he would.

— Mary Hartnett, Wilmington

Helping out with homework

When my daughter, Hannah Chipman (now 20 years old), was a middle school student at The Tatnall School, she came home with an assignment to do a report on a famous Delawarean. My husband and I, both longtime Biden supporters, suggested that she interview Joe. Hannah put in a call to Joe's office and was told that he was a very busy man but that her message would be passed along. Several days later, our phone rang and it was Joe! While he rode the train back from Washington to Wilmington, he proceeded to let Hannah interview him for 45 minutes, taking the extra effort to call her back four times because his phone kept cutting out. Two of his answers stick in my mind. He told Hannah that he was most proud of his Violence Against Women Act and that being a stutterer as a child taught him a very valuable lesson – never ever make fun of anyone and always treat people equally. This was not a campaign speech. This was our Joe, a good and decent man, taking the time from his very busy schedule to help a little girl do her homework.

— Robin Laskey Chipman, Newark

Making it count

My son John went to St. Edmond's Academy with Sen. Joe Biden's son, Hunter. They played on the same intramural fourth-grade basketball team. The games were played on Saturday mornings, and Biden was always there. My son, known as J.P. at the time, had not yet developed into a good basketball player and went the whole season without scoring a point. The very last game of the season was the championship game. The score was tied with only a few seconds to go when a player fouled my son. He went to the free-throw line and, to everyone's surprise, scored the point that won the championship. Biden came down from the stands, lifted my son above his head and said, "Now I know what you were doing, J.P.! You were saving that until it really counted!"

— Ray Walsh, Wilmington

'... But my name is Joe'

My 10-year-old son and I were shopping at the Pathmark on Lancaster Avenue around 9 p.m. in November 2007. I noticed Sen. Joe Biden walking toward us in the main aisle behind the registers. Knowing who he was, I wanted him to stop so I could shake his hand. Not thinking, I introduced him to my son as Sen. Tom Carper. Without missing a beat, Biden said, "Mr. Carper is a nice fellow, but my name is Joe Biden." He then knelt down so he could be eye-to-eye with my son and asked him his name. My son replied, "My name is Joey Noszek," while shaking the senator's hand. Biden then commented on how they shared the same name and told my son it was very nice to meet him. The impression he left on both of us was a friendly gentleman who showed genuine interest in people.

— John Carl Noszek, Wilmington

Dude, where are the goodies?

Rob Ulmer, formerly of Wilmington, worked for Biden's Washington office from 1994-1996. He recalled being asked to drop Biden's golf clubs off on his way back home in the spring of 1995. I arrived at his house after dark. The lights were all out except one by the door and I was a little nervous because I didn't want to startle him. I got out of my car and left my door open. I saw the senator looking out the window, but out of nowhere one of his dogs came bounding around a corner – and jumped right into my car and sat on the back seat. I went back to my car and tried to get the dog out, but the dog would not budge. The senator looked a little confused. I told him I had his clubs and explained that his dog would not get out of my back seat. He laughed and said, "Ha! I guess he wants to go for a ride." The senator and I took over 10 minutes to coax his big furry dog out of the back seat! I guess what I thought was so funny was that world leaders listen to Joe Biden, but his own dog wouldn't get out of my car for him without dog treats.

— Rob Ulmer, Washington

Winning the hippie vote

As a senior in high school in the early '70s, I had my first experience with Joe Biden when I received a congratulatory letter for an award I had won. I thought, how nice, but who is this guy? Soon after, my mother asked me to go to a coffee with her to meet this new guy who was running for the Senate. I did, in full hippie regalia, more or less to embarrass my mom. Still, this gathering of adults intimidated me and I held back. Biden and his team readied to leave and I thought, "Girl, it's now or never!" and I asked, "Mr. Biden, what are your thoughts about women's reproductive rights?" just as he was passing. He turned and said he'd like very much to answer my question, and he had someone get my address and promised he'd let me know his position. A week later I received a postcard outlining his view. I assure you, his view has remained the same all these years. He had my vote. My very first one, done via absentee ballot because I was out of state at college. I was thrilled he won his first election, and proud that I had a part in it. I sent him a note congratulating him this time. Tragedy struck but our new senator soldiered on, and in spite of all that was happening in his life, not two months after he was sworn in, I got a third note from him. I haven't missed an election since. I realized that my vote can do big things.

— Kristina B. Lynn, Delaware City

Inspiration to succeed

My Biden story begins with a field trip to D.C. in 1994. I was in eighth grade at Talley Junior High. I raised my hand and asked a question, stuttering a little bit. I have struggled with a speech impediment all of my life. After answering my question, Biden pulled me aside. He told me he used to stutter but never let it interfere with his goals. Biden added that he would purposely seek opportunities to speak in public. About a week later, I received a letter from Biden, urging me to remember our conversation about stuttering and being respectful to others. I really took his words to heart the following year when I entered The Tatnall School as a freshman and ran for class president. I won and basically served as class president all through high school and college, giving countless speeches and a few sermons (M.Div. from Harvard Divinity School) along the way. Today, I type this e-mail as an assistant attorney general in Delaware.

— Branden D. Brooks

Mary Hartnett of Wilmington shows the purse that Joe Biden recovered from a purse-snatcher in 1977.

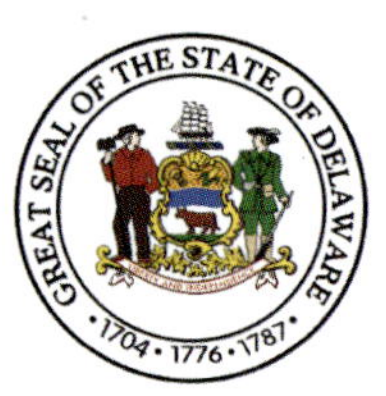

Great success!
Johanna, Vincenzo, Italo, Vincenza, Margherita, Vincenzo Carrieri-Russo
I personally want to thank U.S. Senator Joseph Biden for his support over the years through my campaign with promoting literacy with Success Won't Wait Inc.

—Vincenza Carrieri-Russo
National Jacqueline Kennedy Onassis Award Recipient 2006
Miss Delaware USA 2008

As the next four years will be perhaps the most important time of our lifetime, for the sake of our generation, and our future generations, we wish you much success, much luck, and to you Jill, much happiness in Washington.

—Dale and Sue Lomas

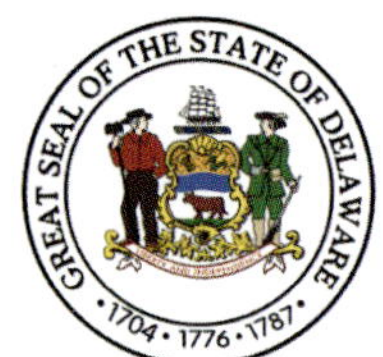

We're lucky. We know what you can do. Now it's time to show the world. Make us proud, Joe.
P.S. Your pledge card is in the mail.

—Your friends at United Way of Delaware, www.uwde.org

MESSAGES TO JOE

... from colleagues, constituents and friends.

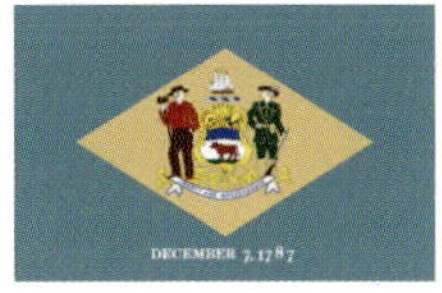

Congrats, Joe! Way to go! My entire family is so very proud for you and of the achievement you succeeded in attaining. I can remember the days of stuffing Christmas cards for your constituents, to you attending Brandywine Raceway functions, to attending crab feasts at my grandfather's house. You have become a staple product of Delaware, accomplishing vast tasks over the years; now the tasks are greater and the stakes are much larger. We have faith in you, Joe. You and President Obama have the talent to turn our country around. God bless you, Joe.

—Michael and Barbara Wirtschafter

The state of Delaware will always be proud to call you one of its finest statesmen. Thank you for your years of service to our country.

—Bill Pyle

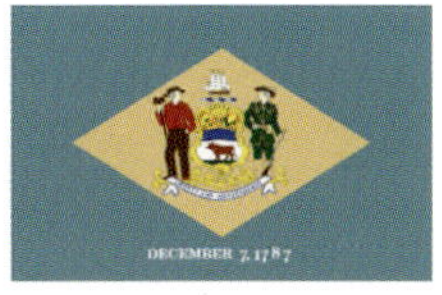

Joe, you have made us proud! As always, we wish you all the best.

—The Emrichs

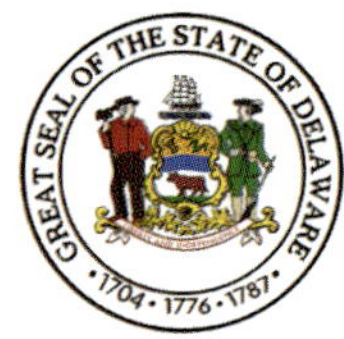

Congratulations, Joe! Thanks for your faithful service to Delaware and best wishes for success as vice president. What an honor to have known you and your family through the years!

—Delaware Secretary of State Harriet Smith Windsor

Dear Joe, 38 years ago, I organized the Blue Ribbon Commission to reform the Democratic Party in our state. As party chairman, I appointed you to this commission. Soon thereafter, Carvel and I gave you the green light to run for the U.S. Senate. No one dreamt a 29 year old could beat Boggs! You surprised us then, and now as vice president.

— Henry Topel

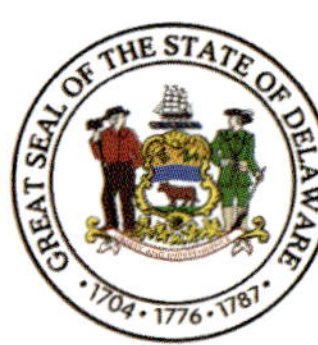

As a former intern (1984), presidential campaign coordinator (1988) and longtime family friend, I am extremely proud to see Joe gain the opportunity to serve our nation at a higher level. But he still has to come back to the Leipsic Fire Hall and serve biscuits at the annual Game Dinner every year!

— John W. Paradee

Our warmest congratulations go to you, Joe Biden, on your election as vice president. Many thanks for your 36 years of service in the U.S. Senate. We all need to follow your lead in service to the country and support your tireless efforts for a strong middle class and a more productive America.

— ***Antony & Sophia Beris***

Thanks, Joe, for all you have done for Delaware and the USA.
— ***Michael & Jean Fusco and Family***

Thanks Joe for all you have done for Delaware and the USA.
— ***Mary Ann Montgomery***

Good luck, Joe! — ***Daniel Martin and Family***

Good luck, Joe! — ***Arnie, Dagmar, Weldin and Carson Dunn***

Good luck, Joe! — ***Linda and Donald Allen***

Good luck, Joe! — ***Sara Jane Weible***

Good luck, Joe! — ***Karen Blum and Family***

Thank you, Joe! — ***Alan & Simone Egler and Family***

Thank you, Joe! — ***Bonnie Klair Kachmar***

Thank you, Joe! — ***Keith B. Short***

Reporter Contributions

Forty years of work by reporters and editors at The News Journal went into the making of this book, including contributions by Cris Barrish, Angie Basiouny, robin brown, Mike Chalmers, Ryan Cormier, Martin Frank, Ginger Gibson, Kristin Harty, Edward L. Kenney, Rachel Kipp, James Merriweather, Maureen Milford, Beth Miller, Jeff Montgomery, Molly Murray, Aaron Nathans, Sean O'Sullivan, Esteban Parra, Jennifer Price, Hiran Ratnayake, Gary Soulsman, Adam Taylor and Nicole Gaudiano.

Photo Credits

Front cover: The News Journal/Fred Comegys

Back cover: The News Journal/Ron Soliman

Foreword

Page 4: The News Journal/Suchat Pederson

Page 7: The News Journal/Suchat Pederson

Page 9: The News Journal/Suchat Pederson

Chapter 1

Page 12: The News Journal/Robert Craig

Page 14: USA Today/H. Darr Beiser

Page 15: GNS/Army Times/Rob Curtis

Page 16: USA Today/Robert Deutsch

Page 19: The News Journal/William Bretzger

Page 20: GNS, Shreveport Times/Greg Pearson

Page 21: The News Journal/Robert Craig

Page 22: Getty Images/Amanda Rivkin

Page 24: USA Today/Jack Gruber

Page 25: The News Journal/Robert Craig

Page 26: The News Journal/Jennifer Corbett

Page 27: The News Journal/Jennifer Corbett

Chapter 2

Page 28: The News Journal/William Bretzger

Page 30: The Biden campaign

Page 31: The News Journal/Jennifer Corbett

Page 32: The News Journal/Jennifer Corbett

Page 33: The Biden campaign

Page 34: The Biden campaign

Page 35: The News Journal/Jennifer Corbett

Chapter 3

Page 36: The News Journal/Suchat Pederson

Page 38: John Walsh

Page 39: John Walsh

Page 40: The News Journal/file

Chapter 4

Page 42: The News Journal/file

Page 45: The News Journal/file

Page 46: The News Journal/Fred Comegys

Page 47: The News Journal/Fred Comegys

Chapter 5

Page 48: The News Journal/file

Page 50: The Biden campaign

Page 51: The News Journal/file

Page 53: The Biden campaign

Page 54: Gannett News Service/Joe Brier

Chapter 6

Page 56: The Associated Press

Page 58: The Des Moines Register/Holly McQueen

Page 59: Iowa City Press/Rodney White

Page 60: The Des Moines Register/Christopher Gannon

Page 61: The Des Moines Register/Holly McQueen

Page 63: The Des Moines Register

Chapter 7

Page 64: The News Journal/Suchat Pederson

Page 66: The News Journal/Ron Soliman

Page 68: The News Journal/file

Page 69: The News Journal/Ron Soliman

Page 70: The News Journal/Jennifer Corbett

Chapter 8

Page 72: The News Journal/Suchat Pederson

Page 74: AFP/Getty Images/Emmanuel Dunand

Page 75: The News Journal/Fred Comegys

Page 77: The News Journal/Suchat Pederson

Chapter 9

Page 78: The Associated Press/Jeff Roberson

Page 80: The News Journal/Fred Comegys

Page 81: The News Journal/Suchat Pederson

Page 82: The News Journal/Suchat Pederson

Page 83: Getty Images/Scott Olson

Page 84: The News Journal/Ron Soliman

Page 86: The News Journal/Ron Soliman

Page 87: The News Journal/Ron Soliman

Chapter 10

Page 88: Getty Images/Win McNamee

Page 90: GNS, The Arizona Republic/Pat Shannahan

Page 91: GNS, Army Times/Rob Curtis

Page 92: GNS, The Arizona Republic/Pat Shannahan

Page 95: GNS, The Indianapolis Star/Sam Riche

Chapter 11

Page 96: The News Journal/Fred Comegys

Page 98: The News Journal/Fred Comegys

Page 100: AFP/Getty Images/Paul J. Richards

Page 101: Getty Images/Don Emmert

Page 102: The News Journal/Suchat Pederson

Page 103: The News Journal/Suchat Pederson

Page 105: The News Journal/Robert Craig

Chapter 12

Page 106: The News Journal/Fred Comegys

Page 109: The News Journal/Suchat Pederson

Page 110: The News Journal/Suchat Pederson

Page 111: The News Journal/Suchat Pederson

Page 112: The News Journal/Suchat Pederson

Page 114: The News Journal/Suchat Pederson

Page 116: The News Journal/Suchat Pederson

Page 117: The News Journal/Suchat Pederson

Chapter 13

Page 118: The News Journal/Ron Soliman

Page 120: The News Journal/T.J. Healy II

Page 122: USA Today/Jack Gruber

Page 123: The News Journal/Fred Comegys

Page 124: The News Journal/Ginger Wall

Epilogue

Page 126: The Associated Press

Page 129: The News Journal/Carla Varisco-Williams